By Jane Hanser

DOGS DON'T LOOK BOTH WAYS

A Primer on Unintended Consequences

Ivy Books

This is based on a true story. The names of certain individuals have been altered or omitted.

My book is dedicated to our owners, our human and canine mothers and fathers, our doctors, the children who love and pet us, the mail carriers who leave us treats every day, and the Animal Control policemen who bring us back home after we've escaped!

The righteous knoweth the life of his beast… *Proverbs*, 12:10

O Lord, How manifold are Thy works! In wisdom hast Thou made them all. *Psalms*, 104:24

THAT'S NOT ME

In some families, little dogs sit on people's laps all day. I've tried sitting on my Dad's lap but he keeps saying, "Ouch! Joey, you *think* you're a little dog but you're not. Get down."

There are also dogs who live in the coldest places on Earth and who run in teams. These dogs work hard, running long distances to help pull heavy sleds over huge fields of silvery snow to transport people and their belongings from one place to another. Well, I'm strong enough to do this type of work, but this isn't me either. When the ground is covered with snow, Mom gets her cross-country skis, and she and I go outside and eagerly walk to The Woods nearby. We descend down one trail into a valley where it levels off and meets new trails and we stop at the base of the first uphill we encounter. She lays her skis on the snow, steps into the foot bindings, attaches one end of the lead to my collar, holds on to the other end, and instructs, "Joey, go go go!" Leading the charge up the hill, I enthusiastically and easily pull her up the snow-covered trail as the lead stretches behind me to its full length. Soon we are almost at the top of the hill. But then I notice some dogs in the distance and those dogs are now much more interesting to me than pulling Mom up the hill is, so I seek the most direct path to the dogs, weaving through the bushes and saplings that impede Mom's person and entangle her in a web of tree trunks and branches.

One snowy day when Mom was gliding along on her skis and I was pulling her around our block, I saw Mary, our mail carrier, going from house to house; with Mom in tow, off I galloped toward Mary to get some of the pocketful of tasty dog biscuits she carries with her in her pockets. What happened to Mom? I don't recall. The last I heard her, she was calling, "Joey, stop. STOP!" and the last I saw her, she was heading right for the hedges. So this type of working dog would not be me.

In other families, people take their dogs out into the fields and then locate ducks, pheasants or rabbits or other small animals for food for the family members. These dogs have very good noses, and after these people have shot the ducks or other small animals, the dogs work hard to help their owners by running out into the fields or swimming out into the ponds to track, locate and retrieve the downed animal. This also would not be me. I view these animals as my friends. Besides, I like my parents to set out breakfast in the morning and dinner in the evening for me. And foods like oranges, chicken, rice, cashew nuts, popcorn, and broccoli are also welcome in between.

Some dogs live in families where they help guide a family member who cannot use his eyes to see. These dogs work hard to assist their partners and masters with walking down sidewalks, crossing streets, going up and down escalators, going shopping, going to work, and coming back home again. This also would not be me. Dogs who do this important type of work sometimes wear a nice jacket that says, "Do not talk to me. I am working." Wherever I go, I like to wag my tail and personally greet everybody I see. When my parents and I are outside walking along the sidewalk, I look ahead and see where I want to go, or with my nose to the ground or pointed into the wind I smell where I want to go, and step down from the curb into the street toward that destination. Sometimes I step off the curb at a spot where another road is crossing. That's when I hear Dad sharply call out, "Joey, stop. Sit. Cars are passing here. Do you want to get hit? Sit until I say it's okay to cross." So I stop and force my body to form the "sit" posture, though my bottom doesn't like to cooperate, hovering and vibrating slightly above the pavement, waiting for some sign that Dad really means what he says. In this position I remain suspended and I plant my gaze firmly on Dad's face, until he looks back at me and repeats even more emphatically this time, "SIT," and my bottom finally and reluctantly cooperates. This I do only because he tells me to.

My parents have a lot of rules for me. They have rules for whether I can jump up on the sofa or not. They have rules for whether I am permitted on their bed or not. They have rules for whether I am allowed to beseech them for food when they are eating, other rules for when they are preparing food, and even more rules for what foods I am allowed to eat, and not eat. They have a rule for where I must sit and wait when people enter our home, and one for who walks through the door first (and last) when we are leaving and entering our home. They have a rule for who goes first when we're going up and down stairs. They have many rules for how I must behave when we go outside. Whether I am allowed past the gate that separates our yard from the world beyond is one such rule. Where I walk, how I walk, how quickly I walk and trot and run when we are outside are others.

When my parents ask me to do something, or expect me to do something, I hear anything from a pleasant sing-song "Good boy, Joey" to an emphatic "Joey, come on! Come on! Come on!" to an irritated "Joey, NO! What did I tell you?" – which is something I hear a lot.

To be honest with you, I don't always obey the rules, but I've learned to put up with many of them, more or less, because with them comes the opportunity to be part of a family where, after dinner, Dad puts on his heavy winter coat, Mom puts on hers, Dad says, "Joey, you don't need a coat. You already have two coats" and then gets my lead, attaches it to my collar, opens the front door and then out we three go, into my promised land, into a cold dark snowy night. All around us the snow is falling so gently and quietly, each dainty flake seems suspended in the air, dancing a silent and unpredictable dance, until it evaporates or reaches the now carpeted ground and lays gently on top of other fallen flakes, or upon my coat, where it nestles, unconcerned.

Dad says that when I was a puppy, I used to try to catch the snowflakes in my mouth. Now, he, Mom, and I are the only ones outside and together off we head in one direction, walking in the middle of the white road. We follow it to where it bends, head up one long small hill as it twists and turns, then up another longer and steeper hill as it twists and turns, and then yet another, where we are so elevated that we can see the tops of trees and the tops of homes all around us in all directions. We cease moving and wonder. I can also pull on the lead and let Dad know where I want to go next, and we walk on, deeper and deeper into the ever expanding world of evening and time and sky and snowfall, closer and closer to the top of the world. I can smell the trails of the bunnies in the snow and though I'd love to follow those trails, I don't. On such nights, I have everything a dog could ever want.

HOME SCHOOLING

Cocoa Brownie was my first teacher.

Breathing heavily, Cocoa Brownie lay in a small, dry, circular, plastic swimming pool that was placed on the floor of the family room and swaddled and padded with cushions, blankets and towels. With bright light from outside streaming in through the many large windows and warming her nursery, nine times she quietly and calmly raised her tail, pushed, gave birth to her litter, and licked each of us clean. Five of us were black and four of us were chocolate. As each one of us emerged with a breath into this world of life and a lot more room to move around, little mama's helper Debra was anxiously waiting there on the scene. She cupped us and held us up high in the air above her head, observed our undersides, and proclaimed, "This one is a girl" or "It's a boy."

We puppies all started out rather tiny and with our eyes yet unopened. I was a small handful of a dog with big ears and a big head, so one day Debra held me warmly in her two palms and raised me up into the air and announced, "I shall call him Big Head." Debra's mom and dad decided that Big Head wasn't such a nice name, so my name was changed to Big Ears.

Mother taught us puppies how to locate and drink her milk and the importance of keeping clean. She taught us to take turns. She taught us to be patient, to have manners, to live with siblings, and to know a mother's love.

Mother was so named because of the rich chocolate color of her coat and eyes. She was American, born in heavily wooded Connecticut. She was a great swimmer. She loved to play in the lake near home, jumping off the dock and into the water with a big splash, and chasing after sticks that her human family would throw. Her human family often brought her to the lake and gave her opportunities to swim and play, and show off.

So it was fitting that we puppies were born in a swimming pool, although one that was dry. We spent much of our time asleep, all curled upon, and warmed by each other and the warm soft curves of Mother and her warm coat, in our plastic swimming pool in the family room. When we were awake, more than anything else we wanted to drink Mother's milk, each of us squirming and pushing against the others to find a good spot. At meal times, often my brothers and sisters used up all the easily available spots before I could find one, so Debra would pick me up, cup me in her hand, then push one of my brothers or sisters out of the way and place me in a spot close to mother's belly where I could get a meal. As the weeks passed, we puppies opened our eyes and began to see our new world. We also grew larger and stronger. That's when Mother taught us how to sit up.

During the day, my human family would allow Mother and us puppies to go outside of our nursery to the wide and sunny world beyond, to the spacious yard, with all its exciting new scents, where we would explore, play, and scamper about in the bushes and in the vegetable garden to everybody's delight, and play we did.

Father was British and he had traveled a long way to the United States and to Connecticut to meet my mother. Though I never met Father, he too was a chocolate Labrador Retriever. Father had excellent eyesight and a superior sense of smell; he was also very obedient.

Father was a champion hunting dog, classified as a Junior Hunter: His owner would go out in the fields and hunt in order to bring dinner home to his family, and Father assisted in this task. Father and his owner, with a pistol in his hand, would walk out to a large open field beneath the wide open sky. In the channels of water of Great Britain, many ducks swam and overhead in the sky many birds flew and rode the waves of the air currents. When Father's owner would stop walking, Father would stop too. Then Father would sit in the tall grass and, despite all the activity and temptations around him, would remain perfectly still. He even kept his tail perfectly still because if he didn't, all the ducks would know that he was hiding somewhere in the grass and then they would swim or fly away to safety and even signal others to do the same.

Father's owner would then raise his arm and pistol into the air, aiming the pistol carefully, and mark and shoot a bird that was flying above the channel. He would then lower his arm. When the bird fell into the water below, Father's owner would again raise his arm, this time without the pistol, high above his head, his now empty hand pointed toward the space above them, and then bend his hand at the wrist to silently signal to Father a direction of travel. Father, carefully observing this, would immediately run in the direction to which he had been commanded, jump into the water, swim in the direction he had been commanded to swim toward, locate the fallen duck with his magnificent sense of smell, and retrieve it by holding it ever so gently in his mouth. Then he would swim back to land with the fallen duck held gently in his mouth and run to where his owner awaited him. There he would carefully and proudly lay dinner at his owner's feet. Father always did just what he was commanded to do, without a sound passing between him and his owner.

Father's name was Buckfold Classical Sir.

I have many championship hunter ancestors from Father's side, and they all have crazy names. One of Father's grandfathers was Bradking Cassidy, whose father was Armadha Mad Hatter and whose mother was Bradking Black Charm, both of whom were Senior Hunters. Senior Hunters could go to the field and retrieve the fallen ducks without even being signaled which direction to run or swim to; they did it purely with their keen eyesight, their superior sense of smell and their ability to focus and concentrate – and their abilities to keep their tails from wagging. Sometimes they were even able to retrieve two different ducks in one effort, a tribute to their remarkable memories.

Great-great-grandmother Bradking Black Charm's parents were Follytower Merry Brook Black Stormer and Bradking Bonny My Girl, both of whom were Championship Hunters. My great-great-great-grandfather Charway Ballywill Will and my great-great-great-great-grandmother, the famous champion Sandylands Tandy, and my other grandmother Sandylands Longley Come Rain were also champion working dogs, on and on it goes, for generations back and back in time with each name getting sillier and sillier and longer and longer. How much time does it take to call, "Follytower Merry Brook Black Stormer, sit!"? Or "Reanacre Mallardhurn Thunder, come"?

But, I find I'm getting far away from where I started out — which seems to be a theme in my life.

There I was, in satisfying comfort, at home with my doggie Mother Cocoa, my siblings, and my human family, learning and exploring the pleasures and excitement of life, and that is also the first time I knew a new type of darkness. We pups were still learning how to sit and were now learning to eat solid food and drink on our own without our mother's milk when, without warning, Mother got sick — they called it cancer — and she left us and never returned to us, her children, her family. But Mother had taught us well. I still had my siblings and a warm and loving home and human family, and our lives went on.

Week by week I started to look less like a puppy and more like a dog. I had long been way too large for Debra's hand. I almost reached up to Debra's knee. I grew stronger. I continued to relish the joy of play with my siblings. I learned to climb stairs and to descend them, especially the stairs that led from our family room to the remarkable outdoors. More and more often our human family allowed us to go into the open air, where I ran in the garden bathed in light, and raced and chased my eight brothers and sisters round and round the wide and tall trees. I also discovered the fun of grabbing onto and pulling at people's shirts and shorts with my newly emerging teeth, tugging with all my might. The louder and longer people laughed and screamed and squirmed, the harder and longer I tugged. I also partook of a joy that was to last for years: the tennis ball. There was a lot of laughter in my first home.

Little by little, however, people began coming to our home and then I noticed that there were fewer and fewer of us puppies. Then there was only my sister and me. Both chocolates, the two of us spent much of the day in the bright sunlight and the cooling shadows. I took care of her, and she took care of me. We were our own little family and we were much too large for the plastic swimming pool. Then one day another man and woman visited and said, "We like her. We like the dark color of her coat," and by evening there was only me.

One morning my human dad opened the front door of our home and he and my human mom went outside to the front lawn; I of course followed behind, wagging my tail. There stood a tall man, a rather friendly man with a smile that went from ear to ear, and a little girl by his side with big eyes, big cheeks and a big smile. She was just about the same size as Debra. I ran right up to her and, because I was almost as tall as she was, started licking her face. She giggled back and picked me up. Then she put me down. I could tell right away that these new people were very good people to follow around and play with.

As I ran about the yard eager to please my new friends and get them to play with me, my first dad said, "He's all yours." Then, turning to me, he said "Goodbye Big Ears!" and gave me kisses.

The new man with the big smile opened his door to the car and my new little friend, who was called Vivi, opened her door to the car, and sat down inside, leaving the door wide open. I jumped right into her lap, which is where I remained for the next few hours. Dad says that I quickly fell asleep and stayed comfortably and peacefully asleep in my new friend's lap and snuggled in her sheltering arms as we sped along the highway. Warm air rushed in through the open windows and rocked me to a deep sleep. When I woke up, the car was stationary, shaded by tall trees, surrounded by fields of grass. This new man in my life had brought me to a new home and we were in Boston, Massachusetts.

By the time the door opened and I darted out of the car and into my new environment, people were looking at me, calling, "Joey." They were looking at me and saying, "Joey, come" and "Joey, sit" and "Good boy, Joey!" So Joey I suddenly was.

And thus I began a whole new life.

Every evening in my new life was capped by sleeping on my new big sister Vivi's soft bed with her and her fluffy pillows; this was reminiscent of Mother Cocoa's warm belly and snuggling up with my little puppy brothers and sisters, except that it was maybe even better. Vivi took up most of the bed, but I had all the space I needed to fully stretch out on top of the covers and make myself at ease. Since I only had to compete with her for space, I was much more successful at it. Lights out was a calming time, a welcome time of togetherness: my new parents would come in to the bedroom and tuck Vivi into bed, give her big hugs and kisses, and give me a big pet. Then the room would be dark. I would close my eyes and abandon myself to reverie.

Once, I'd been stretched out and long in a deep sleep when I was awakened by the abrupt sound of "Joey, come." Who was interrupting my reverie? I saw Dad standing at the door with the hall light behind him. But why? What did he want?

The room was still dark and rapidly shifting my gaze to the window told me it was still very dark outside. Was this the same evening or a different one? Was this the end of one day or the beginning of another? It didn't matter. A young dog has to be ready for anything – and I was. I could smell a new aroma wafting upstairs through the open door, the aroma of Dad's morning coffee, and I was enticed.

I jumped down from the bed without disturbing my big sister, yawned, and stretched my front legs and then my rear legs. Dad turned and walked down the winding stairs, and I followed him down the winding set of stairs, my tail wagging behind me. The rooms downstairs were brightly lit. Now alert and attentive, I followed Dad into the kitchen, where he prepared me a fresh bowl of cool water.

After my drink, he said, "Come on, Joey. Let's go." I'm not sure what he wanted from me, but I knew to follow him around, tail wagging behind me. Then he got the lead, clipped it to my collar, opened the front door and out he stepped into the dark still air of a cool morning not yet formed and yet full of promise. He held the door open for me and to the outside I also stepped and waited at his heels. He closed the front door. Now what?

We walked into the middle of the road. I looked up at him. I was bursting with anticipation but there was a moment's pause in this vastness of colorless forms. The trees, even the sky, seemed to be waiting for some response from him. An orange glow emanated from the tops of tall poles and long crinkled orange and black shadows spread out along the ground where we stood. The road was empty, not another person was anywhere to be seen or heard anywhere. Then Dad turned to face one direction and began running down the open road. Was he chasing something?

"Let's go," he said to me. I followed. I had to, because I was attached to him by the lead. But I kept up. He ran some more, and I kept up. Was I supposed to be chasing something? I guess this was the game. From now on, he didn't speak a word, and neither did I, though occasionally he looked down at me to see how I was doing.

The further we got from our home, the darker it became, and the more I looked up at him for direction and assurance, unaware of the road beneath my feet. I was doing just fine, I sensed. We continued chasing nothing. Dad ran, I ran. He ran down one road, as did I, to the next, passing by the large open field on which sat a large school to one side and heavy woods to the other. As we ran, the school receded into the background and there were new sights to see and new smells. While I didn't have a name for this activity, it took no effort and seemed to be the right thing to be doing. As the road bent, we ran past homes, motionless as we flashed past them. Soon we passed another school and then ran around a big circle which led us to another road. We turned up this road, which passed more homes, and ran up a big hill without even slowing down. I ran, as if I were dancing uphill. Morning's darkness was evaporating; a faint light in the sky was now taking its place, expressing color and revealing the rooftops and yards. Soon I recognized where we were. We were back where we had started out. We were home.

Dad and I remained breathing heavily but were invigorated, and Vivi and Mom were still fast asleep.

The next night I again slept with my big sister Vivi, on our bed. I was sleeping contentedly in our darkened room when standing at the open bedroom door was, again, Dad.

"Joey," he whispered, without disturbing Vivi. "Joey, come." I kept my eyes focused on Dad. He was serious. I jumped off of the bed, yawned, stretched my front legs and then my rear legs.

My tail was now wagging and indicating approval, so Dad turned to head downstairs and I followed him down winding stairs and into the kitchen. I noticed fresh water in my bowl and had a good drink. Then, still wagging my tail, I hovered at Dad's feet while he drank his coffee and had a biscuit. Except for us, our home was quiet and still. Dad fiddled around a little, walked away, and then appeared with the lead that would connect me to him. I was ready this time, anticipating what was to be. He paused only momentarily to look me over and make sure I was ready and willing; the full wags of my tail quieted his doubts.

He walked into the darkness outside, down the path and to the middle of the road, and I followed, and there he clipped the lead onto my collar. After a short pause, his sudden movement, his one, two, three steps in a new direction, broke the hush of the hour. Into the vastness we charged. Our quick legs took us up a long unbroken road to where it bent. The road before us kept on bending and stretching and also elevating higher and higher. Onto another road we turned, and that road too kept on going toward new heights, with trees stretching toward the sky, then onto another road reaching yet higher, to where the tall thick legs of a water tower dwarfed even the tall trees. As quickly as my legs could carry me, the world was expanding and revealing itself in front of my eyes. My breath was heavy but easy. Dad and I continued along the rounding road and back down the hill. I occasionally looked up to him to ask if I was doing what he wanted me to do, and he seemed to approve. The lead connected us but it seemed an encumbrance. The run was spectacular but I secretly wished I could be free and unattached. Just when we were doing a good pace, I often stopped suddenly along the way and explored the smell of some of the aromas that I detected, but then Dad would suddenly stop too and get angry at me. Why? He would tug hard at the lead and indicate we needed to continue moving, and I would acquiesce.

We continued on. A diffuse purple had settled in the sky and on the rooftops, and we were greeted by another dawn just breaking through. Around a large and open park we ran and ran, down the next hill then back up another hill, and there we were again, back where we had begun our circuit. We were home.

Inside our home, Mom and Vivi were fast asleep. In the kitchen, Dad handed me a treat and filled my bowl with more fresh water.

And so began every new morning, roads without end, roads of discovery, and the thrill of arriving home in time to welcome the splendor of the first gentle rays of day and to witness the birds just rousing from their nestled sleep and taking their first flights of the day. I had known the joy of a mother's warmth and the smell of the nourishment she offered, the delight and warmth of eight siblings, the wonder of opening my eyes and seeing the world for the first time, I had known the excitement of traveling to a new place and having a new and loving family. But I was born to run.

As my past receded, my future rushed in.

Then, one morning, several weeks later, the unthinkable occurred.

Our bedroom was still dark, Vivi was sleeping under the covers, I was resting on top of them, listening for the movement and footsteps on the floor beneath me and for Dad to enter the room and tell me, "Joey, let's go." Though alert, I was content to linger here awhile and wait a little longer for Dad to come upstairs. Then I unexpectedly heard the front door slamming shut. I jumped off our bed and onto the floor, leaving my big sister alone in her reverie. I yawned, stretched this way and that, nudged open the door, exited her room, and hurried downstairs to explore. I would find Dad and find out when we were to take our run. I walked through the living room, but Dad wasn't in the living room. I walked into the kitchen; Dad wasn't there. I hurried into my parents' bedroom – the lights were off and he wasn't there either. Puzzled, I sat and waited. My bowl was filled with fresh water, which I drank. Lone morning birds were beginning to chirp. I alone was awake in the home. I waited.

In time, the front door opened and in walked Dad, sweaty and breathing hard. I could smell the outdoors all over him and his clothing. This wasn't right. I wagged my tail furiously, to brush away the bad omen. I tried to block his path to tell him I knew this wasn't right, to beg him it wasn't too late to take me running with him. Then he faced me and looked directly into my pleading eyes and said only one word, "Joey." Then he spoke again.

"Joey, the doctor says you're too young to run."

I behaved as if I didn't understand. I *couldn't* understand this. Too young? Too young to run? What does the doctor have to do with any of this? Who is this doctor, anyway? I had shown Dad how well I could run and how eager I was to accompany him, if not to lead the way! I sat, whipping my strong muscular tail against the floor. I just about came up to Dad's knee.

Then he spoke to me again. "The doctor says I have to wait until you're a little older to take you running with me." This made no sense to me. I was completely perplexed.

Dad then reached for the lead, but it was not a run that he offered: It was a brisk walk.

Thus I faced my next great challenge: I had to save our morning runs together. I had to retrieve our morning runs. I might not be a champion yet but a Labrador Retriever I was, and what's a Retriever without a challenge to be met? I was going to let Dad know what I thought of the doctor's rules. The advantages that I had been endowed with in life, my happy demeanor, my ability to dig holes in the ground, the strength yet gentleness of my powerful jaw, my ability to jump up onto the bed, did not help me here. So I did what I could. Though I was growing larger week by week, I was going to use my small size to my advantage. And if I had to beg, I would beg.

The next morning, I woke up as soon as I heard Dad wake up and fill my water bowl with my fresh morning water. I smelled him prepare his coffee. I was filled with hope that he had changed his mind and was going to invite me running with him. But I didn't wait for him to come get me. I went downstairs to him to make my case.

He was dressed for running and ready to go out the front door. My timing was good. However, again he didn't reach for my lead or call me to the door. I now anticipated the same dreadful disappointment as I'd experienced the morning before, so I approached his feet to block them and his path when he tried to walk, and demonstrated my desire to run. I whipped and wagged my tail and fixed my imploring eyes on him. Failure. Once again Dad went outside without me, saying something like, "Joey, be good," then turning his back on me, closing the front door and leaving me alone, and miserable, in the living room. But I would not give up.

Maybe this next morning would be my lucky morning. Downstairs in the kitchen the following morning, the smell of coffee all permeating the air, I again got under his feet each time he tried to take a step; whether forward, backward, to one side or to the other, I was there first. He would have to notice me and my desire. I continued my protest and appeal. I wagged my tail harder and faster than I ever had. I cried. I sat at his feet, staring up at him. I begged. I fixed my eyes on his. The outcome was the same. Out the front door he slipped, into the darkness, leaving me behind.

I, alone on the other side of the door, felt crushed.

So many subsequent mornings I arose with hope, only to settle into a sense of failure and disappointment. I persisted in my challenge but Dad seemed to prevail yet. The best I could manage to obtain was a slow morning walk, often on the sidewalk, in which we were often passed by other runners and even other dogs.

Once, as coffee was brewing in the kitchen and Dad moved about downstairs, I again took the initiative and went downstairs to plead my case. I again trailed or preceded his movements to block them. For one brief moment Dad stopped moving and lowered his eyes to fix on mine. He was about to say something. But he didn't. I waited. This could be the moment. Then this moment passed. Our eyes met again. *This* could be the moment.

"All right, Joey. You can come with me," he declared. His tone was clear, happy and inviting. This was my first clear victory in life. Dad was no longer thinking about what the doctor ordered.

He got the lead and clipped it onto my collar and out we went. I was wide awake and ready go to, wagging my tail behind me. In the serenity of the early morning, when the dawn chorus of birds was just getting underway, I looked at Dad and waited for his one, two, steps and for him to point the way: Would it be up the road and up the hill, or down the road and down the hill, or up the other road to the other hill? Once we began moving, it didn't matter. We belonged to each other and to the open road.

Each evening, Dad prepared the two of us for the coming day's run: We went outside and into the cool dark autumn evenings and he walked to a spot where the tops of the tall trees did not block his view of the sky and looked up at the sky and tried to locate the moon. When it was a cloudy night, he was happy. When it was a cloudless night, which it was more often, he was also happy but he spoke to me.

"It's going to be a cold run tomorrow, Joey."

Whether or not it was a "cold run" that following morning, there was always excitement under foot. On the open road, the world seemed endless. There was no distance Dad and I couldn't cover by the power of our own legs. We could run as far as we wanted to and as fast as we wanted to, and there was still more to see. There was also more to smell: Every fallen leaf we passed hid a bouquet of aromas, every step revealed a secret about those who had been there before us. Every step was a retriever's dream. And as the leaves began to fall from the trees and then to dry up, there were more and more secrets to discover.

Our three mile runs became longer. Then much longer. We found taller and taller hills to climb higher and higher. My running, always effortless, became even more effortless. I knew what was expected of me, even if I did often stop suddenly to sniff when something irresistible caught my olfactory senses. I grew stronger and larger, my legs carrying me at will. The world became more and more thrilling.

Eventually, the cool mornings of autumn turned into the cooler and darker mornings of my first winter, which turned into the frigid and darkest mornings of winter. Still, yearning and ready, my running partner and I left home and ran for an hour or more. We ran until lights began to appear in the tiny windows of the homes we passed and the newly diffuse light of the morning sky often reflected itself in the blanket of snow on the ground.

"We did some eight-minute miles in that run, Joey," Dad would say to me when we returned home.

Whatever distance Dad ran, I ran. Whatever speed Dad ran, I ran. We ran in the rain, in the gentle snow and in the raging blizzards with ice underfoot. We ran in that cold and in the blazing heat. We ran in the early morning fog and mists. We ran with the wind at our backs, and we ran straight into those howling winds, too. We ran wherever we wanted to. Even better, we would have the roads all to ourselves, while Vivi and Mom were still sleeping, and while you were still sleeping too!

The Labrador Retriever is a strong dog. We are even called "working dogs" because of our ability to work long and hard hours under trying and challenging conditions. We can work in cold and deep water, swimming around fishing nets. We work with ski patrols over the deep snow and with hunters in tall grass and open fields. We work hours on end when necessary. Because we work hard, we must be strong and healthy. When we Labradors begin a new life with a new family, we must be ready and able to fulfill any number of missions in any number of new terrains and situations.

What would be mine?

Long legs help us Labradors move through low brush, and by my first springtime, my legs had grown long, like Mother Cocoa's. Broad and strong chests give us strength and endurance, and mine had grown to resemble Father Buckhold's, the father I had never met.

And so, I very quickly grew larger and, as I maintained my early morning running routine, more muscular and athletic. My weight increased. By the time warm weather returned, I was no longer the little puppy that had scrambled with his eight siblings for Mother's milk. I now weighed seventy pounds.

Still, when my big sister Vivi was ready for bed, she would tenderly say, "Joey, come up" and pat the mattress for me to join her on top of her covers and up I would jump to join her. Then she would turn out her light and the room would darken. It was always a peaceful ending to a happy day. I slept well, especially because with my strong and long legs, I was able to push her and make much more room for myself.

Mom developed a strange new behavior, however: At random times, she peeked her head through the bedroom door and disturbed the silence. "Joey, get down. That's not your bed anymore." I remained in place, ears perked but just staring at her, while my big sister remained sleeping, until again Mom said, "Joey, get down. That's not your bed anymore." Then she would step into the room, pat the soft cushion that she had placed on the floor, and point me to that cushion. "Joey, come," she would again say, and pat the soft cushion.

I was getting larger and larger – but so was Vivi. Why should she get to sleep on top of the soft bed, and I not? I didn't like this new rule. I would oblige Mom with the bed on the floor, at least for a while. At least until she had left the room and gone downstairs. Mom had good hearing but mine was better.

One day Dad discovered he could give me a potato chip and I would gingerly hold it in my mouth as if it were a fragile baby and slowly carry the potato chip to my bed, where I would then sit and eat the chip. Dad was very proud of this ability of mine and this would become a game, Dad giving me more and more potato chips to watch me gently carry them, one at a time, to my bed, where I would eat them. Soon Dad brought people over to our home and had me showing off my strong jaws but gentle mouth and my ability to walk to my bed with my delicate potato chip in my mouth and not disturb it until told to. Soon I had Dad buying bags and bags of potato chips.

Gentle as my mouth was, my jaws became stronger and stronger. I was, for example, able to chew down small trees, some very nice small trees, in fact, that Dad and Mom had planted in our back yard. I had developed the mouth of a true champion Labrador: strong enough to hold onto the retrieve and resist attempts to grab it from our mouths, yet gentle enough to not harm it in any way.

My big ears grew bigger, but so did my whole head. The little puppy who was born with eyes closed and relied on his sense of smell to find his way around the whelping basket to locate breakfast, lunch and dinner was now the large dog whose eyesight had grown keen.

I also developed very good hips and a steady gait. Running long distances had developed strong leg muscles and broad shoulders. I had long forgotten about the doctor who told Dad that I was too young to run.

One early morning I was pleasantly surprised to find another large dog stopped along our route. He stood off to one side of the road, watching us. He was alone. I stopped to explore, which is when Dad, who was connected to me by the lead, got upset. I continued to study my new friend.

"That's no large dog, Joey. That's a coyote." The coyote looked at us, Dad looked at the coyote, I looked at Dad, Dad looked at me, then gruffly said, "I'm getting out of here!" and immediately started to run, yanking me with him and charging forward.

Often, as we followed a long empty road that had woodlands off to one side, Dad would see an orange fox making his way along the perimeter of the woodlands, minding his business. Dad made the rules. "Hush, Joey. A fox."

Another morning brought us to another sudden stop: Dad and I were far from our home and we had just crossed a wide road, lonely and empty at that hour of the day, and were passing in front of a home when we crossed paths and locked eyes with a deer. The deer, startled to see us so early in a morning that he thought belonged only to him, leapt right over a tall fence and out of sight, like the moon rising high above us and fading into the first morning light until it disappears completely.

I met other animals too. At the field by the high school there roamed flocks of wild turkeys and Dad and I always had a good time with these large birds: "Joey, go get the turkeys! Run!" he would encourage me on, and I would sprint after them, only to see them flap their large wings and lift off the ground and fly back and disappear into the woods, where they made their home. Bunnies were always hopping about on the grass, particularly in the early morning, and when they would see me, they would often halt, and then hop away. I desired to play with them and headed their way. But there, Dad taught me another one of my first rules, "No bunnies."

Several times in the grey before daybreak, thundering through the tranquility of the morning, roared the solitary and frightening wail of the fisher cat. Nobody ever saw the fisher cat but we sure heard him. "Joey, get over here," Dad insisted, and he would keep me near him for a few moments to protect me. Then he would turn and run in a different direction, and I would too.

Back home after each morning run, Dad would reach into a jar and pull out one treat – no more, no less – and give it to me. Then he would again fill my bowl with fresh water. I came to expect this wonderful and valuable morning tradition.

My first spring, a period of warmth and light, followed my first winter. The sun sat in the sky for hours and hours and the hard ground started to soften up. One morning, Dad went outside to our back yard and started working. I remained inside but watched him through the large glass door that separated our living space from our yard. A new large wall appeared outside and blocked my easy view of our neighbors' land. Then another wall appeared, connected to the first, then another connected to that. Dad worked on and on, into the evening. Then he opened the sliding glass door that was one side of his bedroom and allowed me to exit our home and go directly into the back yard. That's when I had another new experience: life outdoors but within a fence.

Dad's fence was so tall that I could not see over it. Even Dad couldn't see over it. It was also so low to the ground that I couldn't walk under it. I could, however, partially see through it. I could also hear what was on the other side of the fence and I also could smell what was on the other side.

Eventually Dad and Mom thought I should receive an unnatural education and this involved some games. Most games were fun but this one was very pathetic. Dad got a small object called a clicker, which sounded like a large tree branch breaking, and which was supposed to make me come to them when he held it in his hand and clicked it with his fingers. But I never succumbed to the magic powers it was supposed to hold over me. It startled me, but approach it I would not.

To a dog, an open door is not a metaphor; it is an actual open door. It is an opportunity to run out the door. For me, when I was inside, an open door was also an opportunity to show my Dad who was boss. When I saw an open door, I would run out it so instantly that nobody knew what was happening, then Dad would get the clicker and run outside after me, hold the clicker out in front of him and "*CLICK CLICK.*" So what? Basically, by that point I was gone, the game was on: I called it, "Come get me."

"*Click a-CLICK.*"

Oh? I would look at Dad for a moment, respond, and run, encircling him, faster and faster, always keeping my eye on him. I could cover more ground by running onto our neighbor's land and running circles there, where he couldn't catch me. I infused this game with great vigor and passion and I always seemed to be winning this game.

"Joey," Dad would say again, just the challenge I was looking for. *CLICK a-CLICK.*

Part of the game involved me producing my ferocious bark. The game went like this: *Ferocious bark. Come get me.* I would then stop moving and challenge, my eyes focused on Dad's eyes, my mouth taut, my front legs extended, my back legs dug in fast behind me, and I would emit a low rolling growl followed by several pointed barks. Then my challenger would walk toward me, in seeming victory merely because I was still for a short while, at which point I would launch into more circles and extend the game.

Sometimes it was now two against one, as when Mom would join Dad in trying to capture me. I liked Mom for this reason: She got really worked up when we played this game. This pathetic clicker was useless against my determination to keep the activity going.

Mom would get very angry. I liked that because the angrier she became, the bigger, faster and more driving my circles – and the game – would become. She would get angry when I ran my circles in the back of the home, in the fenced-in area, when Dad was away. She was an important part of my game: To my delight, she would scream at me to encourage me on. "Come on Joey, this isn't funny."

At some point my parents got a little smarter and one of them would get a treat and entice me with that, after which I would give up my game and come back inside, Dad placing the clicker in its spot on the window sill as I walked past its lifeless state of existence.

I suppose there were reasons why my parents didn't want me running my circles outdoors. Maybe there were even some good reasons. But I also didn't care about what they were.

Mom disagreed with Dad about how to talk to me. When I obeyed a command, Dad liked to say "Thank you" to me. Mom, however, thought that was a bad idea.

"Don't say *Thank you* to him. Every time you say *Thank you* he quits doing what you want him to do and starts swinging his tail and heads toward you to give him a big kiss." It was an interesting conversation between Dad and Mom, back and forth and back and forth they would talk. At times like these, Mom was trying to educate Dad, too.

After our morning runs, my morning treat, my morning breakfast and my morning water, I would have to keep myself involved in activity. Any type of activity. Sometimes I would go upstairs to Vivi's bed until she woke up. And then what would I do after she had left home in the morning and Mom woke up? Mom didn't run with Dad and me in the morning and Mom also slept late, even later than Vivi did, and I needed to find some type of work. I found some work, eating the wood from the window sills and eating the shoes that my parents left for me to chew on. Dad was always angry when he came home later in the day and saw the results of my work. Well, that wasn't my problem. I couldn't bring back their shoes and pillows and window sills and socks, could I. Nor did I want to, for I could wait a while and find a new shoe or sock to chew.

Once Mom woke up, she usually stayed home during the day but sometimes she went out. Before she left the home, she would open the big sliding door that connected the bedroom to the back yard and she would let me go outside. Then she would close the sliding door, leaving me out back, and alone. I was supposed to spend the time outside, which was fine with me. I was also supposed to spend the time within this fenced-in area. I was going to learn something about fences, yes, and so was Mom. She was also going to learn something about me.

I spent much of my time sitting outside in the back yard.

I didn't sit just anywhere. Our back yard had a gentle rise toward the back, and a thick, strong and sturdy stone wall that was over one hundred years old ran from one side of our yard to the other. The stone wall added even more height. My favorite location to sit was on top of that stone wall. The fence that my Dad had built lay just beyond my thick stone wall. If I were a king or a prince in the top of a tower surveying all of my lands, I couldn't have been happier than I was there, on my wall. Perhaps Great-great-grandfather Armadha Mad Hatter and Great-great-great-great-great-grandmother Bradking Black Charm had also sat atop stone walls, surveying the miles and miles of estates and fields and valleys before and beneath them, the birds flying from branch to branch above with the wide blue sky as their backdrop. Perhaps they would have loved reigning with me on mine.

By positioning myself solidly on the elevated stone wall I could see our entire yard and beyond. I could see some of the roads that Dad and I ran on. I could also see everything from people strolling up and down the block, joggers, bicyclers peddling up and down the road, children on their way to and from school, Julie the mail carrier delivering the mail, and, most importantly, other dogs being walked. I sat on my wall in the winter when it was covered with snow, in the cool spring, in the hot summer, in the autumn when the leaves were falling all about me.

From atop the wall I could also peer through the rear windows of our home, including the large sliding glass door, and see my parents when they were inside. I could determine if they were looking out at me through a window or the sliding glass door. Sometimes Dad would go up to the window and say, "Where's Joey? I don't see him" and I would turn my head toward him just in time to hear Mom responding, "He's right there." The smallest movement on their parts – a face in the window, a movement through the sliding glass door – and the slightest sound would and could catch my eye. Sometimes it could call off my plans.

My plans were simple. Using my nose, or snout, I would – when I could – nudge open the lock of the gate that allowed people to enter and exit the back yard without having to go through our house. I had seen lots of people enter and exit through this gate: my parents, other dogs who occasionally visited me and played with me in our back yard, their parents... The gardeners particularly liked to use this gate. I knew what was on the other side, I had been on the other side and I wanted to be there again.

Many people underestimate a dog's nose and a dog's sense of smell. They don't ask the question, "Why do dogs have such a large snout?" Dad has a different version of this question: He says, "Joey, your snout is much larger than your brain. I wonder why that is..." And then he proceeds to tell me his answer. He is very intelligent.

This large snout serves many fantastic purposes. First, I can use it to nudge open a gate. It is also like a guidance system, similar to a heat-seeking missile. It picks up a good scent, then guides the rest of me along the path of that scent. As a fisherman's friend, the Labrador Retriever can pick up the scent of a fish. As a hunting dog, that scent can be a bird or a duck. As a pet, that scent could be a child, or another dog! Or lots of other dogs! This is also why I knew when Julie our mail carrier was nearby. I could smell the treats in her pocket long before I could see her. So once I was outside the fence, it really didn't matter which direction I chose to go in. Once I opened that gate with my snout, each direction told a wonderful story. All I had to do was to put my nose to the ground, pick up and follow the scent of another dog, guide myself right to that dog's home, and introduce myself.

The first thing my new friends would do was to look at my collar and say, "Joey Hanser." They were so smart. And the second thing they would do was to telephone my parents. Usually it was Mom who arrived. But until she arrived, I had lots of time to play with my new friend.

One warm afternoon the gardeners came and didn't lock the gate, which I duly noticed, from my vantage point on my wall. Mom was nowhere to be seen and I put my Open Door policy into practice. Using my snout, I pushed up and open the gate fastening mechanism and then pushed the gate wide open. There I was, on the front lawn. I turned left and ambled up the road and up the long hill, continuing to where it turned and kept on elevating. At the end of that road, I found a large park and many children. It was a large park with teachers too and lucky for me it was recess and the children were all outside playing and having fun. That's where I headed and where I got something else that I wanted: attention. Swarming around me, the children asked, "What's his name?" "Can I pet him?"

The teachers, who didn't know the answer to those questions, said, "Well, children, we don't yet know if this dog is friendly." Then they too looked at my collar and said, "Joey Hanser." Mysteriously a few minutes later, Mom appeared in the distance. As my tail was wagging, I saw her walking toward me, and she didn't have the happiest face. I, however, was very proud of how far from home I'd gone and how much attention I was getting – not from Mom, but from the children. Mom was walking a straight and steady line toward me. She got closer and closer. When Mom reached us and stopped, the teachers asked her, "Is he friendly?"

"Joey? Friendly? Oh gosh yes." A smile broke through on Mom's face.

"Can the children pet him?"

"Of course." We were definitely going to be able to remain here for a while with that answer.

And then the children all lined up and, one at a time, each gave me a little pet, mostly on my back or side, then giggled and returned to the end of the line to pet me all over again. The line remained long, with me at its head. I think Mom was kind of proud of me at this moment.

When the line of children had gone around two times, the teachers said, "Thank you" and the children ran off to play, this activity ending as many similar mornings had ended, with Mom clipping the lead onto my collar, walking me to the car, and opening the door for me to jump up and into the back seat of the car.

"Joey, get in." Absent was the fun in her voice. Removed was the smile on her face. Okay, Mom, I get it. I had already had my fun for the day, so I didn't let her get to me. Or maybe I had *some* fun for the day. But why stop at one journey beyond the gate? Why not two, or three? Why not four or five?

Several days later I found my parents had put a padlock on the gate. They showed that they could learn from my experience. But I could learn, as well.

A DEEPENING INCLINATION

Many people ask the question "Why do dogs dig?" and I have given my parents plenty of reason to ask that question and plenty of opportunity to explore the answers to that question. Ever since I was a four-week-old puppy, I was digging significant holes in the ground. My first hole ever was by the side of a staircase that led from our home out into the garden. The staircase, and thus my first hole, was hidden by bushes, which made it an excellent location.

When I was four weeks old and digging holes deep enough for all of my brothers and sisters to fit into, people thought it was funny and cute. "Puppy's diggin'! Puppy's diggin'! Right here!" my first dad screeched with pride and delight in his voice, inviting all to see what I had produced and how my project was getting deeper with each additional moment.

Four years later, I was initiating the same thing but people had a very different response. Why is this? People do change. Shortly after I would dig my hole, I would find Mom had filled it up again. This made no sense to me or to any dog I have ever known, other than perhaps she was giving me another opportunity to dig another hole. My enterprise occasionally paid off in other ways too: One hole I dug made it possible to go directly from our back yard into our neighbors' back yard without obtaining my parents' permission or assistance. I always worked resourcefully, uncovering and exposing large boulders that were hidden under the surface of the soil, dislodging them, rolling them down hills to get them out of the way. This was all work to be proud of. Besides, why should Mom fill up a nice deep hole if I was only going to dig it out again? Why should she worry herself about it and expend unnecessary energy?

There were other reasons for digging, but being a dog I had to learn how to keep some secrets.

My favorite places to excavate have been around the bases of trees and by the sides of our home. A nook or a corner where it is especially shaded or hidden is especially prime. In the summer when the day is at its hottest, I'd also been known to dig a nice large hole. So why do you think we are digging?

It was around the time when I was becoming very proficient at digging when Dad decided to institute a significant improvement in our running routine.

"Joey, if you stay near me, if you obey my voice when I tell you what to do, you'll be able to run without the lead." With an incentive like that, I learned very quickly to run with Dad but to run free and without hindrance. Sometimes I ran up ahead of him and waited for him to catch up; sometimes I lingered behind to smell some interesting scent or mark my territory, and then caught up with him. With my ability to run free, he was no longer afraid he'd take a hard fall if I suddenly stopped to smell something on the ground, which happened often when I was on the lead, and which used to get him very angry at me. Thus, in the mornings I now had the opportunity to use my natural abilities and inclinations, and to enjoy them, even more.

In the afternoons, while I was busy landscaping when Mom let me out back, my parents were making design changes of their own.

One winter, when there was snow on the ground, boxes started to appear in our home. Then more boxes appeared. Stacks and stacks of them took shape. With each new day, new boxes appeared. Parts of our home were becoming fuller and fuller while other parts were becoming emptier and emptier. Then one morning, when I was sitting proudly on my snow-covered stone wall surveying the territory, I saw a large truck come and pull up in front of our home. Naturally I ran over to the fence to see what was happening. Several men got out of the truck and came into our home. Naturally I wanted to greet them so I ran to the back door and caught Mom's attention to let me in. Once I was inside, as much as I tried to get them to play with me and they were saying things like "Yes, I have a dog too" and "Yes, I like dogs," they clearly weren't in the mood to play with me. Instead, they took away all of the boxes and carried them into the truck, and then they took the chairs, the beds, the sofas, the tables. Then they carried away my food, my water bowls and my crate that I sometimes slept in, until our home was as empty as a bird's nest in September. My parents told me to follow them into the car and we took a short ride to a house in a different neighborhood and that house too was empty. When the truck arrived there, that home started filling up with the chairs, sofas, beds and tables from our old home. Then it filled up with the stacks and stacks of boxes, and then the men brought my food and water bowls, and my crate, too, into our new home.

This new home had a nice large yard. The land, however, was flat. It didn't have a superior wall to sit on and to elevate me high above my surrounding kingdom. The land also didn't have a fence to constrain me.

Dad and I soon fell into our morning routine, on new roads, new hills, new trails, around new ponds, along new rivers and new woods. Once again, we set about exploring, one morning at a time, one step at a time, one run at a time.

One favorite place for Dad and me to run was along a very very long and hilly and winding road called the Carriage Lane. This was a very long and old road that also had a long history to it, which Dad would tell me about while we were running its length. "See this, Joey? A train used to run along this very road for miles. When the train went out of business, the track bed was turned into this beautiful Carriage Lane that we are now on." I'd never been on a train so this didn't matter to me.

Mom and I fell into a routine of taking a nice afternoon stroll along the Carriage Lane and around the new neighborhood. In the evenings, Mom would take me out for another walk, when we would see many dogs, with their owners. I made friends quickly and easily in my new neighborhood.

In the late mornings, afternoons, and early evenings, the Carriage Lane was like one large dog park. But it was a dog park with a rule: Dogs had to be on lead. This was a rule that Mom obeyed but that Dad didn't.

Once or twice Mom showed me a statue of two runners that was positioned along the Carriage Lane, and the name of the statue was "The Boston Marathon." This statue didn't mean anything to me: Why should I care about this statue? Did these men have dogs? And if so, did they run with their dogs? That's something I would have been interested in. One Spring day every year these two runners used to run 26 miles with many people cheering them on the whole distance, but Dad and I were running at least ten miles several times a week, often in the rain, usually in the dark, often in the snow *and* the dark, often in the rain and the dark, and always without anybody to cheer us on. It was pure love.

Flanking one side of this Carriage Lane was a wide grassy strip that displayed an array of shady trees and aromatic bushes along its length. Flanking the other side of the grassy berm, the side further from our home, was a much wider road that had a lot of cars going this way and that along it. We never walked or ran on that road. Never ever.

This grassy berm was good for many activities. Some people ran along it on a narrow dirt path that was off to one side. Often when Mom or Dad took me out for a walk, they walked on the Carriage Lane while I walked along this wide grassy berm, my nose to the ground; this was a good location to find and track the scents of the other dogs that had been there before me, sometimes just a few hours before me, sometimes days before me.

In keeping with the custom that Dad had initiated at our old home, he always left the lead at home when he and I went out for our early morning runs. Because the Carriage Lane was its own quiet road separated from the larger road by a wide grassy berm with trees and bushes, he was especially confident that I would be safe from danger. He also began a new routine: When darkness prevailed outside, he clipped little flashing red lights onto my collar. Running in the dark along this road with the lights flashing on my collar allowed me a new sense of excitement and freedom because Dad now allowed me to wander off even further from him and he would not worry.

One of my first new friends in this new neighborhood was the person who carried treats in her pocket: our mail carrier Mary. It was always good to make friends with Mary the mail carrier because she came to our home every day with her pocketful of treats.

Come springtime, when the ground softened, men started working in our back yard, too: Piece by piece, a fence was erected around our home. "Make it Joey-proof," Mom instructed the workers. This new fence was shorter than my other one. I could stand up with my front paws leaning on this fence, but I still couldn't jump or climb over it. This fence, however, was very easy to look through and to look over. I could always see who was coming down the road and those on the other side could see in to view me. I could see dogs being walked, and I could smell them and hear them too, even before I could see them.

My surveys of the fence detected three various exit points, or gates: one in the front, one close to but behind the garage, and one close to the kitchen door. I also noticed that I might be able to dislodge the gate lock with my snout and release the gate and find myself on the other side.

One day I was out in the back yard, Mom was in the house, when – despite having a nice yard to run around in – I decided to see if I could make any progress maneuvering the gate open with my nose. Oh my! Success. I was enjoying myself, walking down the tree-lined sidewalks of my new neighborhood when I saw Mary the mail carrier.

"Hello, Mary! Have you any treats for me?"

"Yes, Joey; I have a treat for you. And, by the way, what are you doing out here? Does your Mom know you're out here all by yourself?" And Mary and I took a little walk, and I followed her and her pocketful of treats every step of the way, right back to my home and up the steps to our front door. She knocked on the front door and, when she didn't get an answer, she just opened the door for me and inside I went, and Mary closed the door and went on her way.

Mom came home through the front door a little later and in an exasperated voice said, "Joey! Where have you been? I've been looking all over for you! I didn't see you out back and I thought you'd escaped!" Moments later she asked me, stupefied, with her voice undulating, "How did you get inside? Where were you hiding? How could I have not seen you?" And we left it at that.

But a few days after that, I found all new locks on the gates, something my parents called "childproof locks."

Labrador Retrievers are not only smart but they are persistent. So if the gate no longer afforded me a passageway to freedom, I would have to find a new way. And I did. I discovered that the soil around our new home was much softer than the soil at my old home, that it was not laden with big rocks, like the soil at our old home, and that I could really dig down deep. My life-long penchant for digging could be very useful here.

These months when the sun stayed longer and longer in the sky and daylight stretched late into the evening, Mom noticed all my excavating and got very annoyed. "How can I stop you from digging?" she asked, angrily waving her hands in the air, as if she were going to throw a ball at me to play catch but didn't. I didn't offer her much consolation or guidance when she asked that question. I really was becoming pretty good at keeping secrets, especially keeping secrets from her.

Sometimes she was successful at preventing me from digging, and sometimes she was not, but my digging certainly kept her occupied throughout the summer months. She spent her time trying to fill up the holes that I had so beautifully excavated, and laying chicken wire on top of the ground along the length of the side of the house and under the bushes. On top of the chicken wire she placed slate and little stones to weigh the chicken wire down. I was happy to spend the time outside with her, really. Still, I always walked slowly and casually to one of my projects, to fool her into thinking I was just going to bask in the sunlight. Sometimes I didn't fool her.

"Joey, come!" she snapped. "What are you doing?"

There were times, however, when she was too late.

Some of my parents' friends are afraid of dogs. When they visit us in our home, children who are afraid of me will hide behind their parents. Adults will get nervous and ask my parents to leave me downstairs in the basement with the basement door shut. I'm not afraid of them, but these people are afraid of me. Some little children are afraid of me because I'm larger than some of them.

Dad and Mom often disagree over what to do in these cases when people who are afraid of me come to our home. Dad wants to put me downstairs in the basement and Mom wants the children to learn not to be afraid of me and how friendly I am. So sometimes I go downstairs with Dad, then back upstairs with Mom, then back downstairs with Dad, then back upstairs with Mom, then I hear them bickering over me and my location, but I remain where I am until my parents make up their minds which it will be. Although I wag my tail with as much affirmation as I can as I try to contribute my vote to their decision-making process, I have no voice in this conversation and usually end up downstairs in the basement, that is, until Mom decides to let me upstairs again. At any rate, once again I am getting off track.

Mary the Postal Carrier with the aromatic pocketful of treats is not afraid of me; in fact she is quite fond of me.

Officer O'Connell is another community friend who is also not afraid of me. He has another name: Animal Control. Every once in a while when I escaped our home or property through some secret means, Animal Control came to where I'd been found, maybe it was somebody's home, maybe it was a park. One spring day I escaped from the yard and walked down along the Carriage Lane all the way to City Hall, where Animal Control was waiting for me. He pleasantly opened the back doors of the Animal Control Police van, into which I jumped; then he closed those doors and drove and drove.

I became very familiar with Animal Control, and the back of his van, this way.

On this occasion, Animal Control stopped and parked the van. Then he stepped out of the van, walked around to the back doors, and opened them, revealing the fact that I was indeed back home, and light streamed in. So did freedom, once again. As I rose to exit the open doors,

Animal Control saw my face and lowered eyes and I saw his face and friendly eyes, and then out into the road down I jumped.

On the front steps of our home appeared Mom. "Thank you, Officer O'Connell," Mom called out, though not with her usual great joy. I noticed that she did not step past the front steps in order to come greet me. I tried to avoid eye contact with her, but it was not easy: I had to get past her in order to get inside. I walked as slowly as I could while still managing to move forward, my nose almost scraping the ground, my tail wagging a slow but nervous low-to-the-ground arc.

I stole a rapid glance at Mom, who was now trying hard to keep from laughing and smiling. Next I heard her turn on her deep, low and monotonic voice, breaking my name apart as if it were two separate words. "JOOOOO - eeeeeey".

Then just when I thought she was done with her admonishment, she started the whole thing up again. "JOOOOO - eeeeeey" once again.

If there had been a way to slink in the front door without having to go through or around Mom or a way to completely avoid eye contact with her, I would have found it, but there wasn't. She wanted me to be sorry for what I had done, but I wasn't. I'd had a good time, I'd made some friends, most recently Officer O'Connell, and I was back home with my family, whom I loved. How could I complain! Or have any regrets?

I couldn't. So I sharpened my ability to leave the premises on my own.

One Sunday morning when a thick layer of snow covered the ground seemed to be the perfect time. By now, though I never understood why not, my big sister Vivi wasn't spending much time at home. In the evenings I was sleeping in the living room, where my parents had placed a new fluffy bed for me.

This particular morning, having heard Dad's alarm clock ring early as usual, I woke up refreshed and ready to go and I sat up, yawned, stood up, stretched my front legs and then my rear legs, crawled along a few steps by pulling myself forward with my front legs, straightened up, and started keeping myself busy. Soon Dad came downstairs to the darkened living room, turned on the light, and found me ready for our invigorating morning run. He ate a biscuit, drank his coffee and I my water, after which we left for our run. The ground was covered with snow. Bright street lights against the dark background dotted our way and lit up the snow that blanketed the neighborhood. Dad was all dressed in his warm running clothes. I was wearing just my own two coats. The longer and harder I ran, the warmer I felt. The pads on the bottoms of my feet kept my feet protected from the cold underfoot and my toe nails gave me traction in the snow so I didn't slip. By the end of our run, a faint glow from the eastern sky revealed a few lone joggers and also a few joggers with their dogs on lead, now starting out and taking our places on the road. If I expressed any interest in playing with these running dogs and slowing down Dad's and my pace, I was met with "Joey, no. Let's go."

Back inside our home after our run, I made my way into the kitchen and over to the treat jar, where I sat, respecting our ritual, and waited for Dad to fulfill his part of our bargain, and there accepted my one treat, as was customary, and carried it softly in my mouth, to my bed, where I lay down and contentedly consumed this edible delight.

Eventually Mom woke up and she, Dad and I were all together.

Luckily for me, later in the day my parents let me go outside into the back yard again. Surely this was one season where they didn't have to worry about me – or so they thought. I'd had enough for one cold snowy winter day, they would assume. Then once again, the spirits of my ancestors snuck up on me. My ancestors could have told me to obey my parents. But instead, they entreated, "Go. Go. Explore and seek opportunity." My long legs, my Mother Cocoa's long legs, would get me through the snow. They would get me anywhere I wanted to go. Somehow, it would work out. I offered no resistance to the call. It was worth a good try.

Cabot Woods is a large wooded area near our home where many dogs like to roam and congregate. Long and winding trails lead high up to the tops of hills and then follow along long ridges, and others lead low down to a ravine that cradles a long boggy pond. The scents coming from that place are overwhelming! Any trail will have a story to tell and to follow. Dogs can run and do run freely in a large open field tucked away in a valley that comes up on us as a huge surprise when we walk there. In the summer, dogs jump into the running water of its long and winding creek to cool off. The Woods is a good place to go on any morning, any day. The Woods was a particularly good place to go on a beautiful morning like this.

The ground was frozen solid and the snow was piled high, so there was no way I could dig. I checked my usual gates for egress and they were all locked. But I did not give up. I discovered one place along the fence behind the garage that showed possibilities. Here, where the chain link attached itself to the top railing by means of small ties, the chain link appeared to be loose. The tie appeared to be missing. A small push on the chain link could provide the key I was looking for. Bushes hid my worksite from my parents' vantage point.

I stood on my hind legs and pressed the weight of my body onto the flexible chain link fence. Within moments, the fence had surrendered. Next I lowered my head under the top rail. Then with a little help from my legs, the collapsed but spring-like chain link fence vaulted me up in the air so I landed on my feet about six feet away from the railing and safely behind the garage. Then I continued the purpose of my journey. It wasn't so difficult after all.

I headed down our driveway to where it encountered the sidewalk and at the road turned right for Cabot Woods. Nose to the ground, on this day I made it to the corner, crossed the road, down another sidewalk, crossed another road. I passed no people along the way. I was approaching my woods. I meandered down the road, a descending and unpaved road that straddles an old stone wall that borders The Woods. Where the stone wall ended was an opening to the park. At the entry I found some dogs. I also found, or maybe she found me, a nice person. And this nice person had a cell phone and decided to do what all the other nice people who I've met do: She looked at my collar and repeated, "Joey Hanser!" We, this woman and her dog and I, spent a pleasant short while together, though she kept me at The Wood's edge and prevented me from entering. Soon there appeared Mom's car, which then stopped, and out of the car stepped Mom.

As that winter slowly melted into a new and warmer time of year, my bed was again on the move: Mom picked up the bed from the living room and placed it on the floor in their bedroom and at the side of their bed.

In the morning after a good night's sleep, I would now be only a few feet from Dad, and a pale light from outside would be filtering into the room, when he would whisper, "Joey, come on. Let's go." Mom remained asleep but I was up, stretched, and ready. This time of year, the world smelled different, sounded different, and looked different, once again. As Dad and I took to the road, the faint light revealed squirrels, bunnies, and other early risers already busy searching for food, as well as various birds high atop the trees or hopping along the ground busy searching for building materials to construct their nests and homes. I was a part of their world, but Dad and I had our own world, too.

In the late mornings and afternoons, Mom let me outside into the back yard, where I sat or reclined in the grass or mulch and welcomed the sensation of warmth and sunlight. The mysterious aromatic world of sweet-smelling freshly bloomed flowers, bushes, and trees drifted to me from all directions.

I wasn't always sitting or reclining, however: I could also be on the move: I might be walking around the perimeter of the fence and out of sight, concealed by the thicket and variety of trees and bushes that bordered our yard and whose leaves were now appearing and thickening.

Under the apple tree was one of my favorite locations to rest. The apple tree's branches spread wide, which when fully in bloom bestowed upon me a wide area of shade, now appealing to me in the warmth of longer hotter days. From under the apple tree I could look over or through the fence toward the street and see and hear who was coming my way. I could also look toward our patio and toward the kitchen door that opened to the patio. I could look directly into the windows of our home and see if anybody was in the house looking at me. I could raise my eyes and look upward toward the second floor deck where Mom would appear from time to time, coming out from the bedroom door and surveying the garden and the world in front of her eyes. Whether I was under the apple tree or navigating the perimeter of our land, I was often either hidden from the scrutinizing eyes of my parents or blended into the surroundings. The brown mulch disguised me, the boughs of the bushes and trees concealed me. The bushes also afforded a strategic advantage: They concealed a favorite spot to dig under the chain link fence.

The best place for me to be situated if I didn't mind being seen by others was to be sitting or lying right in the middle of the lawn, but alas humans must not have very good eyesight because when Dad was inside the house at the time and looking out, he would often say, "Where's Joey?" when I was within plain sight of him. Maybe he just wasn't so used to seeing me so still. Or maybe he didn't trust me. Or maybe I didn't give him a whole lot of reasons to trust me, but I think we'll move on now.

Many times I may have appeared to be sitting and doing nothing but I was not doing nothing. I was sniffing, I was looking, and I was listening.

Mom too often appeared to not be doing anything when, in fact, she was looking very carefully and intently and listening to the sound of low bushes moving as I passed under them as I made my perimeter walk. She was looking to see if I was still there in the back yard under the apple tree or on the soft grass. She would look at me and say, "Joey, if I weren't looking at you, you'd be silently off in the blink of an eye, down the road, in someone's back yard, and out of sight!" She was correct, but even she didn't know how correct she was.

Many of my known ancestors lived together in kennels where they were protected, well-fed, and treated kindly. In the kennels my ancestors were also taught how to behave when out in the field for a retrieve. Other dogs soon became part of the extended family, and other puppies were born who also then became part of the extended family of Labrador Retrievers. I knew a type of kennel too: Every once in a while my parents would put me in the back seat of the car and we would drive to a place near our home that they called The Kennel.

I loved going to The Kennel because I would be around other dogs day and night. So many different dog scents filled the air that it was difficult for me to contain my joy. And sometimes I did not contain it, and people ended up mopping the floor after me. Once or twice during the day somebody would take me outside on a River Walk. It wasn't a run with Dad, it wasn't even a run, but it was nice just the same and I was happy. The walker and I would walk along a path under tall trees and along the banks of the Charles River. On the surface of the river would be ducks, paddling and quacking, occasionally dipping their heads into the water and then raising them back up again, and above were birds flying and gliding. Along the path, runners ran, walkers walked, and bicyclists biked. I occasionally met other dogs being walked by other people, although my walker and I rarely stopped to play and to socialize with these other dogs and people. The air was always fresh, clean, interesting, and inviting, and life along the trail was in constant motion. The path told stories of which animals had passed this way long ago and which had passed this way only recently.

My parents knew that I loved The Kennel. They could tell how much I loved it – and all the other dogs there: My excitement would start to show even before Mom had stopped the car in the parking lot. From the moment I got out of the car, I tugged on the lead with all my might to get inside, without concern for who was on the other end of the lead.

"Joey, stop pulling," Mom urged each time, exasperated. "You're too strong." She wasn't going to give up an inch of the lead, if she could help it, and I wasn't going to stop yanking on my end. Once inside, at the front desk, I would press my substantial weight toward other dogs and Mom would tug back – until one of the men arrived and took my lead, which Mom willingly relinquished, and guided me downstairs to my new and old friends for the next few days. It was always a nice surprise to be brought to The Kennel.

One winter day, when I was nine years old, suitcases started appearing in the bedroom and the living room of our home. Then Mom said, "Come on, Joey. Let's go to the car" and I happily jumped up onto the back seat of the car and once again we drove to The Kennel.

Mom and I entered The Kennel the same as always, with me tugging on the lead, trying to get inside the building more quickly than she would allow. "Geeze, Joey, you're pulling so hard you're choking. Calm down," she admonished, as I raced on ahead. Through the double doors we entered, as quickly as I could.

Inside the large lobby was the check-in counter, in front of which there sat another dog. That was not unusual. But this was not just another dog. It was a chocolate Labrador Retriever, a female, sitting properly and well-behaved at the heels of her parents, who were standing behind her. This chocolate Lab was slightly smaller than me and was looking right at us. Mom just stopped. Moving *and* talking. In somewhat of a trance, she seemed to forget all about me. I stopped tugging and opted to, instead, just wag my tail. Mom's eyes locked into the eyes of this dog, who just stared back at her, and then growled a little, at her, but not at me. What was going on?

This female Retriever was being protective. But why? And who was she growling at?

When another dog growls at me, I like to back off. Mom, on the other hand, took a small step closer to the Lab. The Lab growled again. Mom took a step closer. I waited behind her, wagging my tail. The dog's parents held their dog even close to their toes. Who were these people? How close was Mom going to get? Then Mom looked up toward this Retriever's parents and blurted out, "How old is your dog?"

"Nine," they responded, another sign of friendship. I was glad they were getting along so well.

"Where was your dog born?" Mom pressed on. By now she had really forgotten about me.

"Connecticut," they responded.

And then she said it. "I think these two dogs are littermates."

Thus it came to pass that, after nine and one half years, I was reunited with my sister and littermate. I came to be reunited with Rosie.

After our Mother Cocoa had passed away and all the other siblings had found new homes, Rosie and I had remained the last two unclaimed puppies of the litter. The two of us had spent our September days wandering the sunny garden together, running, frolicking, and chasing each other. Together, we two chocolates learned to play with the newly fallen leaves, and to chew on tree branches. My sister wasn't called Rosie then, and I wasn't called Joey, but together we had learned the joys of being born Labrador Retrievers and the joys of discovery.

And so there in The Kennel lobby, our parents did what they do so well: They continued talking and jabbering. And looking at us.

Rosie's mom and dad said things like, "Wow. Rosie has Joey's eyes!" and everybody agreed. Rosie's dad pointed out that both she and I had on the same type collar and how well it matched our brown coats, and Mom agreed. Rosie's dad and mom also agreed and offered: "Let's plan on getting the two dogs together for a family walk and reunion in the springtime." And springtime wasn't too far off.

The kennel supervisor, who was now observing all this, came up with his own plan. "I can have Rosie and Joey in pens side by side" for all the time we were both in The Kennel. "They can get to know each other again that way." It was agreed, and I went downstairs with the kennel worker wagging my tail and for all of that week spent my time next to my sister. It wasn't exactly like old times, but it was close enough.

As the kennel supervisor led me away to my temporary home, Rosie's parents could be heard still talking to each other, saying, "Wow. Do you think that Rosie recognized Joey? She was much friendlier to him than she usually is to other dogs."

Mom was busy asking, "Do you think that Joey recognized Rosie?"

Either way, I'm certain that Mother Cocoa was somewhere, smiling at our good fortune.

The Big Dig

Digging had its special challenges when all eyes were on me. But when nobody was looking, all the other dogs and rabbits in the neighborhood seemed to call in unison: "Joey, Joey . . . Come join us . . . You belong here, with us . . . Dig here . . . Now . . . " Though audible to me, Mom and Dad couldn't hear these animals calling, however, and I took advantage of that.

Very warm weather had rolled around once again. Small flowers were popping up all over the gardens, injecting the air with their sweet floral scents, and lining the curbs of the roads. Small leaves had appeared on the trees and birds had returned from their winter destinations. The ground was softening. Once again it was prime digging season. And once again I saw a too familiar site in our home: suitcases.

Dad's suitcases were out once again, on the floors, on the beds, and he was filling them up with things – his things. Later that night we all three got into the car, which thrilled me, and went for a ride, another opportunity to smell the wild wind thrusting itself into my face through the open window, and ended up at the airport, at which time Mom got out of her side of the car, Dad got out of his side of the car, lifted his suitcase out too, and came around to my open window. I eagerly waited for him to open my door, but he didn't. Instead, he said, "Joey, be good." Then he said, "Joey, don't be a jerk," leaned his head through the open window, gave me a kiss and let me give him a bigger kiss. Then he kissed Mom and uttered, "I'll miss you" and off he walked, with his suitcases, into the airport as Mom came around to the other side of the car, sat in the driver's seat, closed her door, and drove us away.

The evening was a cool and cloudless night in March, a nearly full moon hung motionless high above the rooftops, and if Dad had been home, he would have proclaimed, "It'll be a cold run tomorrow."

This evening I slept in my bed, and Mom slept alone in hers.

The following morning at daybreak, I was a wreck. I was fidgety. The scents from blossoms opening and my busy animal friends filled the air and aroused my senses. I wanted Dad's alarm clock to ring at 4 o'clock in the morning and Dad to wake up like he usually did and put on his running shoes and I would follow him downstairs and outside he and I would go, and he would choose a direction, and away we would run with a burst of fresh energy. But the morning had broken, birds were awake and singing their songs, morning colors filled the sky, and there was no Dad to wake me up and invite me to go running with him. I arose, stood by my parents' bed and extended my head over the mattress top: Mom was there but she was asleep. I lay back down and waited. Daylight had begun filtering into the bedroom and still Mom had not budged. The door was slightly ajar: I went downstairs on my own. Soon the sky was a bright blue, squirrels were screeching and jumping from tree to tree, cars were on the road and whirring by, our home was warming up, and still Mom had not stirred. I had to respect that, even if I was anxious. I climbed the stairs, went back to the bedroom and in my anxiety banged my strong and wagging tail around on the furniture and walls and produced some noise. Then, like the wind in the trees, Mom stirred and finally and calmly arose.

"Good morning, Joey. Okay, I'll let you out. Let's go... Let's go downstairs." And she slowly emerged from her bed and walked down the staircase with me following a few steps behind her, my tail wagging behind me. She made her way to the kitchen, then to the sun porch, and opened the door to the back yard, with me brushing past her legs as I made my way down the three steps into the back yard. As I walked away from her and our house and toward the garden, I heard the back door close. She was going to leave me out here alone. If I couldn't see Mom, maybe Mom couldn't see me. This morning might have possibilities yet.

This might have been a good morning for me to sit under the apple tree, whose new leaves provided some shade. It might have been a nice morning to lay on top of the soft ground and the spring grass and close my eyes and go back to sleep basking in the cool morning light. I tried both of those. No. I was yearning and restless and itching for my morning run, yet Dad was nowhere around. And it was the season for dogs.

The chain link fence along the back of our yard might provide the answer. So might the evergreen tree planted in front of the fence that stood in between the kitchen and me that blocked Mom from seeing what I was up to.

Labrador Retrievers are essentially hunters and fishers. We are trained to run long distances to retrieve a bird that has fallen, or a water animal that has swum from the fisherman's net, and in order to do this we must be able to conquer any obstacle we find in our way. We may need to run over land, swim through water, run along the edge of a pond, swim again, run back along the land around a clump of bushes, swim, run across a road, run across land, swim again, retrieve an animal that we have never seen before, hold it gently in our mouths, and bring it back to our owners and handlers unscathed. We may need to swim for long periods of time in cold, deep water. Many of us are also trained to smell the onset of diseases and alert our owners to the possibility of harm long before our owners know they are ill. Almost no challenge is too great for a Labrador. Generations of Labradors have been praised for their abilities to work. So, on this particularly beautiful morning, when some Labrador Retrievers were working in the fields and others were working to help their owners get to and from work, when other Labradors were saving lives and others were running in fields, I needed to get busy.

On this morning in my neighborhood, when the air lifted and carried the scent of the animal life from one block to another, from one yard to another, when vegetable gardens were attracting bunnies and fresh berries on trees were attracting the birds, when children were chatting and walking to school, birds were perched high in the tops of the tall trees, some singing to each other and some busy building their summer nests, others looking for food for their families, and other dogs were out being walked by their owners, on this morning when Dad was missing for our precious morning run, I set about *my* work.

My four strong legs, strengthened by years and miles of running, led me to my spot by the chain link fence where I smelled that a bunny had passed through earlier that morning. This would be my point of departure.

Mom had previously placed a wooden plank along the perimeter of the fence in order to block me from access to the bottom of the chain link fence, where I would be prone to digging. The wooden plank I easily pushed aside.

With the plank pushed aside, I identified the spot for me. The spot faced the direction of the early morning light so through the opening between the ground and the bottom of the fence I saw my way. At first, I dug slowly, testing the ground to see if it was soft enough or still hard from the winter. It was soft enough. I dug more quickly then and the hole became deeper and wider, then deeper and wider. I was forced to dig even deeper in order to get under the thick immovable solid bar that ran along the bottom of the chain link fence. My strong front legs pulled. Then my head and nose followed. And my hind legs pushed. I squeezed my thin body into that space under the bar of the chain link fence, pulling with my front legs, pushing with my back.

At this point I encountered another challenge. Six inches behind our fence was another taller and solid wooden fence that I hadn't planned on. The solution presented itself. Between the two fences was just enough room, a gap of about six inches, for me to squeeze my thin body through and about thirty feet later I would be free.

I nosed my way up and into the small gap in between our chain link fence and the solid wooden fence that lay only a few inches beyond that, turning slightly to the right as I squeezed through. My thin body now through that narrow gap between the two fences, the chain link flexed as needed as I pushed with my rear legs and slid my way through for about thirty feet to where both fences ended. I was free.

Once free and upright, I kept my nose pointed to the ground and walked up our driveway toward our street. I was pleased and in good spirits. At the end of our driveway, just like Dad always chose one direction over another for our morning, I too could choose a direction. I could go toward The Woods, or I could go toward the wide grassy berm of the Carriage Lane.

Keeping my nose to the ground, I picked up some scents that interested me. Numerous dogs had already been along my block that morning, I could tell. Their appealing scents guided me safely down our block toward the Carriage Lane. As I approached the corner and the open space, I raised my eyes to see the Carriage Lane coming into view. This was good timing: I noticed a group of dogs, and people, off in the distance in the direction of the pond.

Slowly I stepped into the road, entered the Carriage Lane and headed toward the group of dogs, still nose down, swinging my tail behind me. What a perfect and inspiring morning this was turning out to be. To my left flank was the grassy berm that separated the Carriage Lane from the larger and busier avenue where the cars headed to and fro, where I never walked. I was almost at the group. I looked up, my tail swinging more and more quickly. And finally, I was there!

A neighbor was walking her dog along the Carriage Lane and she and her little dog joined up with the group of dogs and people. The neighbor, seeing me coming toward her – and off-leash and all alone – and toward the other dogs, all of whom were on lead, was feeling neighborly that morning. Fearing that I would get hurt, she suddenly moved toward me and extended her hand to reach for my collar.

Excuse me, do I know you? was my first reaction. *You're not my Mom or my Dad* was my second reaction, if one could separate the two reactions, which took place in rapid succession. My instinct worked very quickly and then told me to run in exactly the opposite direction from her. Which just happened to be across the berm and into the wide street with all the cars.

Almost simultaneously I felt the darkness and the pain everywhere, and I let out a big cry. And another cry, and another.

What had hit me? It was a bright morning, but I couldn't see anything but stars.

Immediately, everything became busy and dizzy and noisy. I crawled away from beneath the car. I crawled to the berm. The people who were walking their own dogs along the Carriage Lane rushed toward me and were trying to catch me. The bright morning sun was now throbbing. The person in the car started to cry. I feel sad when people cry but I was in my own pain. I maneuvered through the crowd and through the bushes by the side of the berm. The sanitation workers who were driving their large trucks stopped their trucks and got out to see how they could help. One person on the grassy berm got out her cell phone. I think she was trying to call Animal Control. The sanitation workers were trying to find me. Everybody was trying to help.

But I was trying to run away.

On this day I didn't stick around long enough to wait for my friend Officer O'Connell to bring me back home in his nice clean white van.

Hurting all over, in all the commotion I slipped through more bushes and ran across the Carriage Lane, across people's lawn, down the street, and then another, toward home.

I could no longer hear the birds sing. I couldn't hear anything sing. I could barely see or feel the ground beneath my feet. But I knew my way home. Home stood there, patiently waiting for me. I made my way down the long driveway to the back of our home and turned toward the gate that opened into our back yard. The gate was shut. Darn. I couldn't go back in the way I had come out. I would sit here outside the gate and eventually Mom would notice me. So I sat upright and faced the gate, faced our home, faced my hopes that Mom would find me sitting there, and I waited, and shivered. Mom would notice me.

Time passed. Time crawled. Time stopped.

I continued to wait. And sit. Mom will appear. I will sit here and Mom will appear and see me. I will sit here and Mom will appear and take care of me.

The waiting dragged on. The silence dragged on.

Then when the world was a big blur, there was the sharp pop of a door opening. It was the sound of Mom opening the bedroom door to the second floor deck above me. Then there was the second sound, that of her footsteps as she walked out onto the deck and stood by the railing. She would look for me in my usual morning spot under the apple tree, where I should be camouflaged in the mulch. Then she would call, "Joey! Joey, come!" And I wouldn't come. Then there would be a long silence. A long pause. I would just wait right here until she noticed me, here on the driveway.

Looking upward to the deck railing, from my place by the gate, I followed her eyes as she looked outward, toward the apple tree – and just saw grass where I should be. Then I saw the pause. She hesitated. I then followed her eyes as she deliberately focused them to follow the perimeter of our yard, slowly from the front to the side to the rear. Her face was solemn. I followed her eyes as they inevitably turned downward along the other side, the side nearest my present location, toward the three stairs that would be below her. As her eyes turned downward, she saw me. Her eyes had met mine.

She didn't voice it aloud but I know what she was thinking. She was thinking, "Joey, why are you on the wrong side of the fence?" She was searching for an answer, but found none. She thought again. "Joey, why are you on the wrong side of the fence?" An answer wouldn't come to her, and I didn't offer her any suggestions, but as she looked down at me she calculated that something wasn't right. Something was, in fact, wrong.

Mom then disappeared from my sight, the kitchen door opened, the sun porch door opened, and she reappeared directly in front of me, at ground level, at my level. She pulled open the chain link gate and came to me. She crouched by my side. I wasn't kissing her morning kisses as I normally would do. My tail wasn't wagging as it normally would wag. The chain-link gate now opened, I carefully stood up and moved a few feet in, toward the "in" side of the gate. Mom then closed the gate, I was now securely inside, and she knelt before me, carefully and gently examining my legs, my chest, my paws, my head, and noticing my shivering. She looked into my eyes so intently that I could almost hear what she was thinking. She pet me, took my paw gingerly in her hands, and looked at it, looked all around my chest and four legs.

Then she left me there and went inside. While I sat and waited outside, Mom was inside on the telephone. "There's an emergency with Joey. No, I don't know what happened. Maybe a wild animal, but it's a little too late in the day for wild animals. I'm bringing him over right now."

I remained in the same spot. I didn't feel cold; I don't know what I felt, actually.

I heard her get into her car and drive it down the driveway toward where I sat, and then I saw her get out of the car and open the rear door of the car. Turning toward me, she opened the back gate again and walked me toward the car, wrapped a towel around my chest and belly, then lifted me up, trying to avoid all the areas where I was wounded, which was difficult, and put all eighty pounds of me in the back seat of the car, which is a pretty big deal. *Whatever you say, Mom. Today, whatever you say.*

Then off we drove. I didn't tell her what had happened to me. And she didn't ask. Things were pretty quiet in the car all the way to wherever it was we were going.

HANDICAPPED PARKING

Dogs don't typically tell people – or even other dogs – when they're in pain. Some people say this has to do with our pack animal nature. Dogs in the wild lived, and live, in packs, in groups. Frequently the group is a family, a mom and dad and the litter, the children, that stays together until the children grow up and form their own new families and packs. But as life in nature, one weakened or injured dog in the pack slows down the whole group from animals who are predators. As you can imagine, no dog who is injured wants the other dogs to know this because the pack needs to keep on moving, and the injured dog doesn't want to get left behind.

I, on the other hand, didn't live in the wild, nor had I ever. There I was, living with a nice family, in a nice home, and protected by my loving and caring parents. My Dad had even gone to all the trouble of putting up a fence for me to keep me safe. It had worked, until I did something wild and impulsive like digging my way out from the yard and taking a leisurely walk to socialize with other dogs and get some exercise. Yet here I was behaving like a pack animal living in the wild, keeping my pain to myself.

When Mom and I arrived at the animal hospital, my hospital, a place where I'd been countless times before, where I knew and loved all the doctors and doctors' helpers and they me, she parked the car right up front in the "Handicapped Parking" spot, and broke her silence. "Okay, Joey. We're here." As if she had to tell me.

Then she got out of the car, closed the car door behind her and, leaving me alone, ran up the ramp and into the hospital. Alone in the backseat of the car, I didn't try to climb into the front seat and pretend that I was the driver.

In a moment two technicians were running out of the hospital carrying a stretcher between them, scampering down the ramp toward our car, and putting me onto the stretcher. "Easy. Easy," they were saying. Then, working together, the technicians carried the stretcher, with me on it, up the ramp and into the hospital. So this is what emergency parking was all about. For once I didn't get to enjoy the promenade from the car to the front door, along my way taking in all the scents of other dogs and cats who'd been there before me and stopping to contribute my mark, usually a tug of war between Mom on one end of the lead and me on the other.

Once I was inside this hospital, the veterinarians carried me straight to the back room, a private room where only doctors and their patients are allowed. There the veterinarians gave me oxygen and fluids so that I would feel better and calm down.

"Good boy," they said. They checked out my heart and lungs.

"Good boy," the doctors said again and again. Those words always soothed. I stretched my neck and gave the doctors some kisses, which seemed like the right and natural thing to do. It also made me immensely popular among the staff there. Before I knew it, I'd been given shots to calm me down so I wasn't in pain. Every once in a while, Mom's face appeared in the little glass window that was set in the door separating the waiting room from the treatment room, looking in on me. Then her face would disappear.

That's when Mom was agonizing in the hospital lobby, alone, wondering how I had gotten hurt.

Had I been hit by a car?

Coyotes are nocturnal animals and where coyotes roam, many people who have cats won't let their cats outside at night. In our suburban but wooded neighborhood true stories were told of coyotes who lived in the woods and who came out of the woods to the roads and streets where people live and have their homes. The city officials tell people who have cats not to leave cat food outside, lest its smell attract the coyotes. Last month our neighbor was walking her little dog after dark and she saw a coyote on the Carriage Lane. A coyote can easily hurt a dog, especially a small dog, and will. My parents saw a coyote one summer night on somebody's front lawn as they were driving down the road.

Had I been attacked by a coyote?

The wild turkeys roaming our street in late summer and autumn are particularly fun to watch – and even more fun to chase, when Dad (rarely anymore) lets me. The turkeys come in flocks of eight or ten, and they peck and peck their ways from one lawn to another, not bothering anybody and keeping to themselves and their flock. Some are babies and some are full-grown. Dad saw one fly over our fence one time and in October Mom saw three fly up to our roof and remain there awhile, doing what I have no idea, then she saw them very gracefully fly down and land in the road in front of our home, then continue on their unhurried way. When I am out running with Dad I often pick up their scent and start to head off in their direction. Dad doesn't know what's going on for a while – until he sees them. When this happens Dad stops wherever we are and says, "Joey sit and be quiet," so I do. He doesn't want the big birds to be frightened and to run suddenly into the roads.

Deer have also occasionally wandered out of the woods by themselves but when they see other people or animals, they are more interested in finding their way back into the woods, or at least a wooded place. Usually when I am out running with Dad and he sees a deer in the early morning, he is so stunned with the great size of the animal that he just stops and stares while the deer, also stunned, prances off with a great leap and avoids the curious and startled stare of our watchful eyes.

And there, alone, Mom paced and wondered: Had a wild animal come and attacked me? In the daylight? Was this possible? Had the fence come alive and grabbed me and done me harm?

Soon, one doctor came out from the surgical room into the lobby, approached Mom and looked her straight in the eye. In a quiet voice, the doctor said, "Your dog has been hit by a car. You need to get him to Angell immediately." Two utterances, in quick succession, without time for Mom to comprehend either one.

There was a brief pause during which time Mom said nothing and did nothing – nothing other than fixing her eyes on the doctor's eyes.

"What's Angell?" she returned.

"It's a hospital in West Roxbury."

"Can I go later, like in a few hours?" Mom asked. She was thinking of the dinner she had to finish cooking for a big celebration that was coming up tomorrow night.

It was a standoff that the doctor was ready for.

"If you don't go right away, your dog could die" is what the doctor said, in a quiet and steady voice. But what Mom heard was: "If you don't go right away, your dog could DIE."

In a moment the technicians at my Animal Medical Center returned me to the stretcher and carried the stretcher, with me on it, back out to the reception room where Mom was, then carried me on the stretcher outside to Mom's car, with Mom following, and put the entire stretcher, with me on it, onto the back seat of the car. "Easy. Easy," they again said, though I wasn't hearing the words, which I don't think were intended for me anyway. In fact, I wasn't hearing anything. Maybe I was hearing the sound of the headache in my head. Then Mom and I drove off and she drove and drove; we were headed somewhere, certainly not back home, with me lying on the stretcher on the back seat.

On and on we drove. Things were happening so quickly. Being reclined on the stretcher in the back seat, I couldn't see much, but then again I wasn't interested in looking out the window. I couldn't stretch my head out an open window to enjoy fresh air, nor did I want to. I could feel the car turning and driving, then turning, then driving still further, then driving over a bumpy road, and turning again. The silence in the car was probably welcome. There was only me and Mom. There was only the two of us and the silence between us.

Angell Animal Medical Center is a large animal hospital, open twenty four hours a day for all types of animals and all types of medical emergencies.

When we arrived at this new place, Mom again parked right up front in the "Handicapped Parking" space, then ran in to the building, leaving me again alone in the back seat of the car. Soon, another group of technicians appeared, this group rolling a gurney with them, a big long table on wheels, to the car, reached into the car and pulled the whole stretcher with me on it out of the back seat, put the stretcher with me on it right on top of the gurney, and quickly wheeled me into this large building with large doors that opened automatically.

"Is this Joey?"

It was a little late to be asking. If I wasn't Joey, then who did they think they were they rolling into the hospital?

A lot of new things were happening to me, new people, new places, new ways of getting from one place to another, new feelings. And they were all happening very quickly.

NEW DIGS

The Labrador Retriever has become so popular because we are smart, gentle, athletic and we live so well in families like yours. Ever since the forerunner of our breed, the St. John Water Dog, a small and mighty fishing dog that worked hard off the cold waters of Labrador as early as the 1700s, was discovered and brought to Great Britain in the 1800s, where we were bred and became a distinct breed, we Labs have gotten along with everybody. We have become popular in Great Britain, in India, in the United States, in Canada, in Australia. We have become popular where large bodies of water are present, and where large and open fields abound, where it is hot and where it is cold. We like people who are short and people who are tall. We like people who have no hair on their heads, and people who have a lot of hair on their heads – like us. We don't care! We like people who like us and we even like people who don't like us (as long as they are kind to us). And so being at the Animal Medical Center was, for me, like being at a wonderful party, with new people for me to love, new dogs with their owners and parents for me to explore, new doctors and technicians, and even new cats arriving all the time, though the cats were always in little carriers so I couldn't get up close to know them.

I felt secure in this large medical center. But on this day I was also feeling really sick – really sick, very weak and very groggy. I definitely wasn't feeling like myself. And yet I was also feeling rather relieved that the worst was over.

"Kiko Bracker," spoke my newest friend, a tall man with an easy smile, to my Mom much later that day, as he entered the hospital lobby from the treatment rooms and extended his hand to her. "I'm Joey's emergency physician."

I spent that day and the next six days here in my new home away from home and little by little when I woke up in the morning I would actually know where I was. The road back to knowing how I got here in the first place was a little less in focus.

On my first few days there, Dr. Kiko and other doctors took good and immediate care of my injuries. My belly had been badly injured as it scraped the ground, and the doctors paid a lot of attention to that. My ankle had been broken; they paid a lot of attention to that. Three toes of my left leg had been broken, and they paid a lot of attention to them. In order to treat me, the doctors shaved my entire left side. They took x-rays of my leg but I was so good and never whimpered and always sat so perfectly still that they never had to anesthetize me, something that Dr. Kiko was very proud of. I was unaware of what was happening around me for much of the time. Then I was aware again and something new and stiff was on my left hind leg. This, the splint, kept my ankles and toes in a proper position and protected them from being touched or knocked so that they would heal properly. Wrapped around the splint were bandages. When I walked, I would hold my injured leg, the leg with the splint, up in the air and hop on my three good legs.

If I had been able to ask him, I would have pleaded, *Dr. Kiko, can you and I please go for a run?* And when he wouldn't answer, I would plead, *Dr. Kiko, can you and I please go for a little walk?* although honestly, I was so groggy in the beginning that mostly what I wanted to do was to sleep and even going outside for a pee was a major effort. Dr. Kiko paid a lot of attention to me and I sensed that he too had a dog at home and that maybe he and his dog even went running. I gave Dr. Kiko lots of kisses too and a few additional kisses to take home with him.

When Dr. Kiko would take me for a walk around the medical center, other people would look and say, "Congratulations on your wonderful new patient." The attention was always welcome and boosted my spirits. I may have had a broken ankle but my tail was doing just fine.

The hospital attended to my dental needs too. An animal's history and diet determine what type of teeth he has. Dogs have some small teeth called incisors in the front top and bottom of their mouths. These teeth help the dog to scoop the little pieces of food into their mouths to chew and also help us dogs to groom ourselves and stay clean. Dogs also have 'canines,' which means 'dogs': two large and pointed teeth in the top and bottom set of teeth that help us to grip onto food and other large things, such as treats. Like humans, dogs also have premolars and molars. When I am holding a potato chip or a pistachio nut in my mouth, I am usually holding it between my top and bottom molars, but very gently – the mark of a fine Labrador Retriever. Now I would have a new mouth: One upper canine tooth and two upper incisors were broken from the accident, and one day during this hospital stay my doctor and I walked into another medical room where I fell fast asleep and when I woke up, those teeth were gone.

With three fewer teeth in my mouth, my parents were worried, wondering how I would eat. But a dog will always find a way to eat.

For my sleeping arrangements, I had a nice private pen in a room with many other pens, each of which was occupied by a different patient. Because I was a large dog and had an injured foot, I was on a bottom row. Most of the day I spent in my pen, inside which were also small machines and lots of tubes. It was a bit crowded in there, but I wasn't in the mood, or able, to move around much anyway. Often the doctors were coming around and checking up on me. Several times a day somebody came and led me outside to a small and grassy park for a walk. Or perhaps for a hop. Three feet, hop. Three feet, hop. This sequence took some getting used to.

One morning, I was in my pen, feeling groggy and dazed, somewhere halfway between asleep and awake, although I fortunately didn't have to choose between them. I could sleep if I wanted to sleep, and I could look about if I so wanted. I couldn't remember the last time I'd seen Mom. Actually, I couldn't remember much of anything. I hadn't seen Dad in days. And then in my semi-slumber I imagined – no, I heard the distinct sounds of Dr. Kiko's and Mom's voices.

I strained to raise my head and pried open my heavy eyelids and there – through the haze and the fog in my head – I saw Mom standing before me. Her presence registered slowly.

"Joey! Hi Joey!" Her voice was soft and trembling.

Yes, it was Mom. *Thump thump thump* my tail managed. Dr. Kiko bent down and opened the door to my pen. *Thump thump thump* was the sluggish refrain of my tail once again.

Mom then traded places with Dr. Kiko and bent down so low that she and I were eye to eye; now at my level, she crawled right into my pen, brushed right past me, right past the IV lines and the heart monitor that were in my pen, sustaining me. I could not even turn my head to follow her, I was so groggy. With my ears I followed the path of her movement. She continued crawling until she was behind me. Once there, she made a little place to sit right up against me. She gently placed her hand on my head and patted me. "Good boy, Joey. Good boy," I heard her softly say. I don't know what I was doing that was so "good." Lying here unable to move my head? Lying here unable to even give her a kiss? I could sense that she wanted to cry. But she held back her tears and I sensed her trying to push through a smile.

How does a dog sense these things – love and comfort, danger and trouble, fear and apprehension – without even a word leaving ones lips?

There were other patients in the Critical Care Unit too, each one also in his own pen, a temporary dwelling which offered us security and safety, and these patients also had visitors. But a little girl whose dog was a patient in the pen next to mine was upset, complaining to the doctor. "I think he's very unhappy here in this pen in this hospital," she said, sounding unhappy herself.

"Dogs are not like people," the doctor explained. I could agree with that. "They are quite comfortable in their own pens and sometimes away from home."

As the doctor uttered those words, I dozed off again. I awoke to detect Mom squeezing past me again and past all the equipment again, and when she was in front of me, she kissed me gently on the top of my head, gently slipped through the little pen's door, softly closed it, and whispered, "Joey, I love you. See you soon."

As Dr. Kiko's patient, I started feeling stronger and better day by day.

One morning, as I lay groggy in my private pen, Dr. Kiko came to my pen and opened its door. "Good morning, Joey!" He fiddled with all my bandages and told me to come out. Out of the pen I walked, or hopped, awkwardly, accustoming myself to the abundance of space around me. Then Dr. Kiko put a plastic bag on my injured leg to cover my splint, which covered my entire leg, so that my bandages would not get wet – and there were many ways in which I could possibly get my bandages wet. Then he attached my lead and we went for one more proud and short walk, my tail wagging behind me the whole time.

We walked through the halls of the private domain of the hospital, where all the doctors and the medical rooms were, then through a set of large double doors, and right into the public domain, with its large, open and sun-filled main lobby. The lobby today was filled with dogs, cats, hamsters, rabbits and snakes, and parents, little brothers and little sisters of dogs, cats, hamsters, rabbits and snakes but what I noticed was not the animals. There, to my surprise, sat Mom and Dad! I hadn't seen Dad in ages, and there he was! This was the best surprise of all. He stood up, headed straight toward me.

"Joey! You look great!" he exclaimed. And I felt great.

Dr. Kiko looked happy and proud. Then I heard Dad utter that question, "What's that?"

Dr. Kiko immediately went into a long explanation as to why I was shaved bald on my entire back, my entire left side and my entire left leg. Smiling the entire time, he also demonstrated how to remove the plastic bag from over my splint and how to put it back on.

He then handed my lead to Dad, and Dad and Mom turned to face the large glass window that revealed the outdoors; in step with them, I walked happily out of the hospital into the fresh air, which now felt considerably fresher on the left side of my body. I was wagging my tail as we walked to our car, though everything, even that, took more effort than usual. I could not, as I used to do so easily, jump up onto the back seat of the car. Dad now had to lift me up and put me on the back seat to protect those parts of me that were still hurt and broken, and there were many parts of me that were hurting and broken.

HOME AND NOT ALONE

Home looked and felt warm, wonderful, and safe. It also looked different.

I too looked different from the morning of the day I'd tunneled my way under the fence and out to freedom. I didn't mind this difference; I've never cared about how I looked. What I minded was being and feeling miserable in my own home. Home was where I belonged, and I was happy to be home, but I was also miserable. Moving from place to place or room to room was not the free and easy thing I was accustomed to or that I wanted it to be. Forget about running. I walked – or hopped – slowly, using three legs, holding my injured leg, with its splint, up in the air so that it didn't touch the ground.

My bed was once again situated in the living room, but the living room also looked different. The furniture was differently arranged so that when I was on my bed in the living room and my parents were also in the living room, I could always see them, as long as my eyes were open. I could also, from where my bed was now situated, see the barricade of chairs that my parents had constructed at the entryway to the living room.

My food and water bowls were now located in the living room, just a few feet away from my bed. This was nice and handy when I was thirsty or hungry, but there was a downside. After I drank and ate, if I stood up and started to walk any further, such as toward the doorway, my parents seemed to be right there, commanding, "Joey, NO. Go back to your bed." There was another difference: Not only was I not allowed to leave the living room but I wasn't permitted to leave the immediate area of my bed. *Oh, come on, Mom and Dad. Please change your minds. Please let me walk out of the living room.* But my pleading was to no avail. My methods of pleading also changed. I couldn't run around them or violate the barrier of chairs. The best supplication I could manage was to look at them for as long as I could hold my head up and not blink. There was no doubt: This discussion was going to go their way.

At first, my food was also different. For my first few days back home, I was only fed rice because my mouth was sore from the dental surgery and rice was easier to chew than my regular dry food.

My parents were also now reading something called The Instructions, which told them what kinds of medicines I had to take and when, each day, I had to take them. There was Day 1 and followed by Day 2, Day 3 and Day 4, and so on, until Day 9. This Day 9 seemed to have some importance because my parents were always saying, "Day 9."

The tones of my parents' voices were also different. Instead of one saying, "I gave Joey his treat," the morning now sounded something like this: "Did you give Joey his meds this morning?" or "I didn't feed Joey this morning. Can you give him breakfast and then give him his meds?" I hated the meds. I hated when Dad would firmly say, "Sit" and I would, obediently, then looking intently into his eyes or following his hand expecting a treat or a piece of an orange or something delicious, I would find myself tricked, as Dad would quickly wrench open my jaws as I fought with all my might to keep them closed, shove his hand into the back of my mouth, drop the med down the back of my mouth and so very quickly remove his hand, shut my jaws closed and hold my mouth closed – as long as it took – until I swallowed this pill. On the other hand, The Instructions said to "Always give after a meal," which meant that twice a day my parents would fill my bowl with some appetizing food that I was sure to want, which began as rice and which by Day 8 had thankfully turned into chicken or turkey. There was a good side.

I heard a new question: "Will Joey ever run again?"

I was asking myself a similar question: "When will I run again?" And I was dreaming of it.

I had to dream of it. Dad no longer woke me up early in the morning to go running with him. He now woke me up in the morning, saying "Come on, Joey! Time to go out!" *To go out* –

but not to run. Dad walked me one or two blocks and then turned around to come home. And stay home. It hurt to walk, but it hurt differently not to run.

Still, I wouldn't complain. Although I wasn't running, the early morning open air belonged to Dad and me.

Mom had a new morning routine. Until now, after she woke up every morning and headed downstairs, she would go into the living room and open up all the shades and let in light from outside and then head into the kitchen. Now, when Mom came downstairs in the morning, she no longer came into the living room, opened all the shades and let in the sunlight. She also never drew the living room shades in the late afternoon. In fact, the shades and curtains in the living room remained drawn all day. The evening lasted all day. My parents made it impossible for me to look out the windows and see dogs and people walking by our home. Doctor's orders, they didn't want me to get too excited or to jump up on the sofa.

With only one top canine tooth now, another challenge was how to grab onto the treat my parents gave me after each of my morning walks. Just as I had found a way out of our back yard on so many occasions, I would find a way to grab onto that treat, and to eat it, as the doctors had predicted.

And so, each day, despite my darkened living quarters, my clunker leg, and my having to take meds each day, I learned new tricks and new skills. Some parts of this were like back in my first home, when I was a puppy in Connecticut and learning to open my eyes and see, then learning to use my legs for the first time, to eat solid food for the first time, to climb steps for the first time. And each new day – especially when in the early morning I would smell Dad's coffee in the kitchen and from my bed be able to see him quietly walk past me wearing his running clothes and head for the front door and our grand outdoors – I hoped and longed for the morning when I could take my place by his side, again.

I'm sure that at night while I was in my bed downstairs in the living room and Dad and Mom were upstairs in theirs, the conversation went something like this:

Mom would ask, "So, how do you feel about this?"

"I miss my running partner," Dad would reply.

I was in the living room in the midst of my suffering and social isolation when, one afternoon, a truck pulled up to our home. The doorbell rang. A man stood at the door. I wasn't permitted outside. I couldn't even get past the barricade of chairs that blocked my entry into the hallway. But at least I could still *bark* and my bark could travel anywhere and break through any barriers. So bark I did! Then Mom allowed the man passage into our home, and he delivered something – a large and heavy carton – and left. I resumed my barking.

"Joey, knock it off. Be quiet." Mom clearly wasn't happy with some aspect of me. She wanted to deny me the one joy that still came so easily to me. I continued to bark.

My family had had many home deliveries but this home delivery was different. Because Mom would not allow me out of the living room, I could not even catch a glimpse of the delivery man. "I'm sorry, puppy. I'm sorry," said Mom, sympathetically, as she continued fidgeting with the box. But neither her tone of voice nor her words – and certainly not her actions – were very convincing or consoling.

Mom then pulled the large carton into the hallway right by the wide doorway that opened into the living room. I waited in the living room as close as I could get to her and she removed the barricade of chairs that separated us. There was hope here.

She opened the large box. She pulled out something that smelled of wood. My eyes grew wide. My tail started to tick like a metronome. It's perhaps a new toy for me! Next, she got a screw driver, sat on the floor, and started working. And working. I wanted to play with her, and with this new toy, and I let her know this by wagging and wagging my tail. I'm saying *Oh, please please please let me out to play with this new toy* as hard as I can! But she kept working, focused on her task. Now and then she tried to make me feel good by using another name she had for me and saying "Hi Jo Jo!" and also smiling at me and waving to me from only two feet away, but it also wasn't working.

She and I weren't going to play together and this wasn't a toy for me.

About one hour later, there was a little wooden gate set up in the doorway to the living room that I could see through but that was too high for me to jump over. I was stuck on one side of it. I couldn't push this obstruction away or figure out a way to open its little door, though Mom and Dad seemed to have no problem opening its little door and walking right through. This was a huge frustration for me. A dog gate was not my idea of a toy. This time I think my parents were too smart for me. Being stuck in the living room had, I think, something to do with following "the doctor's orders." This spatial limitation was the hardest part about recuperating. Could it get any worse?

The answer came soon enough: Yes, it could.

On my Day 7 visit to Dr. Kiko and the Animal Medical Center, I came home wearing a new object, a new thing, around my neck. My parents call it a cone. I did not like this cone. Dr. Kiko called it a collar but I think he was just being the kind, kind person and animal lover that he was. The Instructions called it an "Elizabethan collar." But do I look like my name is Elizabeth?

It was very wide and stiff and blocked my view of everything above me and below me and to all sides of me. When I walked, it bumped into things and prevented me from progressing in my path. When I ate, it bumped into my food bowl. When I drank water, it bumped into my water bowl. Sometimes I even had to wear it when I slept.

So why *was* I wearing it?

"Joey, I know you don't like to wear this but it will protect you," Mom and Dad said.

How will it help me?

"Your wounds need to heal." Doctors wanted the stitches in my belly to heal properly, they claimed. Cone or not, I had my own ideas.

The most difficult time of the day was the evening. In the evenings, Dad was back home from work but I still had to wear the cone *and* I was confined to the one room, the living room, thanks to the new un-toy. But my parents understood my longing, and many evenings they came into the living room and sat down on the sofa and talked to each other but faced me, just so that I was not so alone and so that I could see them. Sometimes they brought their dinner into the living room and ate their dinner there too. These evenings I could sometimes walk over to them and receive pets and give kisses.

Most of the time, however, when I stood up to be closer to them, stretched, and started heading their way, there would be an unpredictable but decisive and dispiriting, "Joey, go to your bed" and I would lower my head, turn around and sulk my short way back to my bed.

Once my parents knew I was lying down in my bed, they made sure that they rubbed cream into my sore belly, which had been injured in the accident. If I wasn't already wearing the cone, this is also when they always made sure I was wearing it.

Each evening, they kissed me on the top of my head, gave me a pat on my head and maybe kissed the top of my head again and softly whispered, "Good night, Joey. I love you." I would watch them turn away, watch them get smaller and smaller as they headed away from me and out of the room, and the room would become suddenly dark. And I would fall asleep.

One evening after dinner, Dad got a book, sat down in front of my bed in his rocking chair and started reading to me.

"Once upon a time," Dad began, while my head was resting on my bed but my eyes were wide open and raised up to see him, "in a place called New York City, there was a beagle named Alex. Alex, just like you, Joey, was always very excited when his mom would take him outside to walk along the busy sidewalks of his neighborhood. Alex would be on the lead while his mom walked him past many cars and buses and trucks. They would walk to the end of one block where they, along with many other pedestrians, would wait at the corner, until his Mom said, 'Go, Alex' and then they would cross the street. On and on they would travel, from one corner to another, stopping and waiting, and then starting again, this happening again and again, until they reached a large green park called Central Park. There, Alex's mom would take off his lead and allow him to run around with the other dogs who also lived in New York City and played in the Central Park.

"One day Alex's mom unclipped Alex's lead at the Central Park, like usual. Alex played and ran and chased other dogs until he was breathless, like usual, then played some more. He found some interesting smells along the ground and followed them, just like a private detective. His mom waited for him to return to her, but he did not return. She called out, 'Alex! Alex, come' but Alex did not come. She ran across the field to where some other dogs were chasing each other, but Alex was not among them. She called, looked and ran. It was getting later and later and still Alex did not appear. Concerned, Alex's mom walked home alone, looking everywhere.

"She got to the block she lived on and arrived at the doorstep of their home. Something small and brown with large ears was sitting there, looking up and wagging his tail. 'Alex! It's you! You walked all the way home – without me! I'm so glad and thankful that you're safe and sound. Come; let's go inside.' And she opened up the front door and a happy beagle walked inside, followed by his happy mom."

I listened to the sound of Dad's reassuring voice, until I closed my eyes and trailed off into a deep, relaxing sleep, and dreamed.

DOGS DON'T LOOK BOTH WAYS

Mom has one story that she has repeated many times, usually before she feeds me. "Many years ago, our father Abraham was sent a servant named Eliezer out to another land to look for a wife for his son, Isaac. Eliezer traveled far away and into a distant land with ten camels for the journey. One evening, he approached the wells, where the city limits were, and had his thirsty camels lie down and wait there for somebody to come and draw water for them.

"In a little while, a woman named Rebecca came with her water pitcher, drew water, and offered it to Eliezer. After he had finished drinking, she returned to the well and drew more water, this time for Eliezer's camels, until they too were satiated."

Recently she told me this story again, and I recognized a few words in that story, like 'drink' and 'water.'

"And so, Joey," Mom continued, "I always have to be kind to you and make sure you have plenty of food and water."

Mom was in charge of making sure I ate my breakfast and dinner. If I wasn't hungry, which was often, she tried to make my breakfast interesting for me by adding some chicken soup to it. Sometimes I refused to eat my breakfast. I would stand there, sniff around, look around, look up at her, face my food but roll my eyes toward the floor then toward her to see if she was looking at me, then stretch and sniff around again. I'd do anything but eat.

And then she would say, "Joey, eat your breakfast."

She would keep her eyes pinned on me the whole time. I hated that. Some people think that dogs don't speak or comprehend speech, but I understood exactly what she wanted from me. She wanted me to eat my breakfast.

Mom was also in charge of making sure I ate my dinner in the evening. Again I had no appetite, and Mom would feed me my dinner and try to make it interesting by pouring some chicken soup into it. If I didn't eat it, she would say, standing above me, "Joey, eat. Eat your dinner" in some weird monotone. Then she would alter the tone of her voice to be sweet. Either way, either voice, she would keep her eyes on me the whole time. I hated that. She is really good at that, good at staring at me. If I stared at her and she stared at me, she usually won. "Aha, Joey. You blinked. I won," she would laugh. She was having fun. But this game she played because she wanted me to eat because I couldn't take my medicine on an empty stomach.

Many people say that dogs don't speak or understand English, but I understood exactly what she wanted from me. She wanted me to eat my dinner.

Then there came a bright morning when I was to take a car ride and see my friend Dr. Kiko again. This was the day my parents had been talking about, Day 9 of The Instructions.

What I loved about going to see Dr. Kiko was that I could leave our home and be outside for a little bit longer than usual, move around a lot more, and take a pleasure ride in the car. Also, while I was in the car, I didn't have to wear the collar. Mom opened the window by me, and while the car was moving I'd sit up close to the open window, close my eyes and feel the sensation of fresh air blowing on my face. I'd take a lot of quick sniffs and be swept away by all the lovely scents in the air. It was as if I were running as quickly as the wind, or the wind were running to catch up with me. Days like this gave me hope that Mom would take the collar off and never put it back on again.

 Soon I was at the Animal Medical Center.

Whenever I am at an animal hospital, I am unaware of which animal is big and which animal is little. Some dogs are on leads like I am, some are in carriers. On this Day 9, there was one dog who had three legs and he was hopping around, as happy as could be. The whole experience of being in the hospital was wonderful. Any one of these dogs could be my friend! Though I was always on the lead while in the lobby, sometimes Mom permitted me to play a little with these dogs. My nose, eyes and ears were always active, sniffing, scouting, listening, and my tail wagged continuously. Lots of dogs, including me, were quick to mark the walls and posts in order to say to each other, in our own language, "I am here!"

Each time that I went to the hospital, the doctors wanted to know how much I weighed, whether I'd gained or lost weight. "Stay still, Joey," they repeated. Oh how I hated to sit on the surface of that scale and remain still. As soon as my rump touched the scale, I would stand up again. Dr. Kiko needed to know my weight so he could figure out how much medicine I should be taking.

In the two weeks since I'd been hit by the car, I'd lost weight. I'd been a strong and muscular eighty pounds. Today I weighed seventy pounds. "That's because he isn't running," Mom said, and Dr. Kiko agreed with her: It had been two long weeks since Dad and I had run together. And so after that day, Mom started keeping a record of my weight, which told her when to feed me more food, and when to feed me less food.

After I stepped off the scale that morning, Dr. Kiko brought me to another area for my examination. *He* allowed me to walk a longer distance than my parents had, and he enjoyed it. I felt my strength and my spirit returning with each step.

In the hospital, the stitches and staples that the doctors had put into my leg and my belly during my first emergency visit were removed, but I was more pleased by the fact that my doctor allowed me to be free of having to wear the cone. He re-bandaged my splint so that it was a bright blue.

After my examination, Dr. Kiko brought me back to the lobby where Mom was waiting with her list. "I have a lot of questions, Dr. Kiko," she said. And she took out a little piece of paper on which she had written her questions. Here in the lobby, Mom sat down and I, being on a short lead, sat on the floor by her. Dr. Kiko stood nearby, and the two of them talked and talked, mostly about me.

The talk about me, "Joey" this, "Joey" that, "Joey" and more "Joey" held little interest to me. There were other dogs that were walking in and out of the hospital, with their owners in tow, and that was the world I then cared about.

There were often times when I was frustrated that I couldn't follow my parents' talk. There were often times when I was frustrated that my parents couldn't understand me or understand what I wanted. There were times when my parents were similarly frustrated.

"What do you want, Joey?" There was frustration and tension in those words. "I don't know what it is you want."

I would look at them, my brow furrowed, trying hard to make some sense of their message, trying hard to explain to them what exactly I wanted. I would look at Mom, then at Dad, then back at Mom, hoping to unlock their secret. Between their world and my world was a divide that we both tried, often unsuccessfully, to cross.

One world that neither of us understood about the other was the world of color and colors. We just saw things differently. I love to lie down on the yellowish purple grass of our yard. Yellowish purple? Well, that's what I see – not the green that my parents see. I also love to play catch with dull yellow tennis balls. Dull yellow? Yes. I don't see the bright yellow that my parents see. The bright blue bandages that Dr. Kiko wrapped around my splint this morning, if I cared about the color of the bandages at all, which I didn't, appeared to me as a dull blue color. But what did this color matter to me anyway. I was much more allured by the world of scents.

So while in the hospital lobby and Mom and Dr. Kiko talking away, naturally a little girl who was there came over to make friends with me. She was very happy and curious, and petted me and made me feel very happy. Then she turned to Mom, who was still talking, and asked, "What happened to him?" The little girl continued to pet me.

"He was hit by a car," Mom said.

The little girl appeared puzzled. "Didn't he look both ways when he was crossing the street?"

It was a rare moment when Mom didn't know what to say. Then words found their way back out of her mouth. "No, dogs don't look both ways." Her eyes briefly blinked. "Dogs also don't pay attention to traffic lights or to stop signs."

But why don't we?

If that's true, how, then, do guide dogs know when to cross the street?

And why did it take Mom so long to realize that my world looked completely different from hers?

The world is full of many colors and many questions.

LEGWARE

"Joey, Joey, look at me," completely baffled me. What did she want from me? Little by little Mom started getting some kind of camera apparatus bug. This was some sort of new game to her and a game that only one of us – and I wasn't the one – thought was fun. I would have to sit. I would have to stay – and stay. She would face me with this camera object held tightly in her hands. And then what? It was absolutely the most boring and pointless game I could imagine. Sometimes I would be doing such a good job of sitting and staying and she would say, "Joey, your tongue is hanging out. Put your tongue back in your mouth." What would be the point of that? Dogs perspire and regulate their body temperature through their tongues so this was a request that went against our nature.

There were more adjustments in the days following my return home from the hospital. I was particularly thirsty so it's a good thing that my water bowls were still kept full of fresh water at all times.

I detected a unique smell in my food in the morning and again in the evening, maybe a new type of medicine. I didn't like this new aroma and I didn't want to eat. So Mom poured a little chicken soup into each meal. "Joey, eat." Mom was being rather nice to me at mealtimes now.

There was new trouble, too, after my big Day 9 check-up.

My parents seemed concerned that I was chewing away at the bottom edge of my splint. I acknowledge that I was chewing away at the bottom edge of my splint, but did they have to be *so* concerned about it?

When my parents first saw this new behavior, Mom right away called out, "Get a sock" and Dad came to us with one of his running socks in hand and slipped my leg, with its splint, into the sock. This would protect my toes and the sock was a perfect fit. If I couldn't be running with Dad, at least I could dress like a runner.

Later that evening, Dad came close up to me, removed my running sock, examined my toes and feet, and said my "toenails need to be cut." Then Doctor Dad proudly proclaimed, "Since he's not running, his toenails aren't naturally being kept short" and his diagnosis continued, "and his toenails on his injured foot are pressing on the splint and irritating his foot so perhaps he's chewing the splint to make space for his longer toenails." Perhaps.

The next day Mom and I had another delightful car ride back to the neighborhood animal hospital to test Dad's theory. Along with my usual bandage change and the usual cleaning of my wounds, I got a nice pedicure on all four feet.

This seemed to work for a few days.

When all was calm in our home, I quietly renewed chewing at the splint, only this time I made more progress with it. Again, Mom had me wear a clean running sock that she'd gotten from Dad's drawer, and again I got a boost up and into the back seat of the car, and again off we went on another car ride to the neighborhood animal hospital. Like usual, I loved the drive. The opening of the rear window delivered invigorating aromas to me that brought me back to my senses. Who cared where we were going!

Our destination this time was the little animal hospital. This was not bad for an otherwise irritating morning. This time Dr. Tamara came out to attend to me and my chewing on my splint. She was one wise doctor.

"He's trying to tell us something," she explained. My parents had not understood that I was trying to tell them something. Or if they had, they certainly didn't understand *what* I was trying to tell them. Dr. Tamara, on the other hand, was trying to understand my language and to understand exactly what I was trying to communicate. Was I trying to tell her that my foot was itchy? Or that my foot or leg hurt?

She unwrapped my bandages, took my temperature, and generally checked me out. She discovered that I had an infection in my toes and that I was chewing away at my bandages because my foot and toes itched and I wanted to get some relief.

Back I went on more medicine. I couldn't see any advantages to taking this medicine or see any reasons for having to open my mouth wide, or more accurately to having my mouth opened wide, then having somebody – namely Dad – reach his hand into the back of my mouth and put a tiny little pill on the back of my tongue, then having my mouth held shut until I swallowed the pill. What was the point? The only point I could see was that when all this was done, Dad always gave me a treat. All my irritation would be forgotten.

I liked the way it had been before – when Mom would put my pills in a little piece of bread and roll it all up in a little ball that I would then take out of her hand and eat – because I love bread. So what happened? After about three weeks of doing that, Mom suddenly discontinued this. Maybe that had something to do with my reaching for the kitchen counter with my front paws and eating the bread and cheese that she had left unattended?

The sad part for me was that this evening, the cone was back on. I love my doctors and I love my parents, but was this progress?

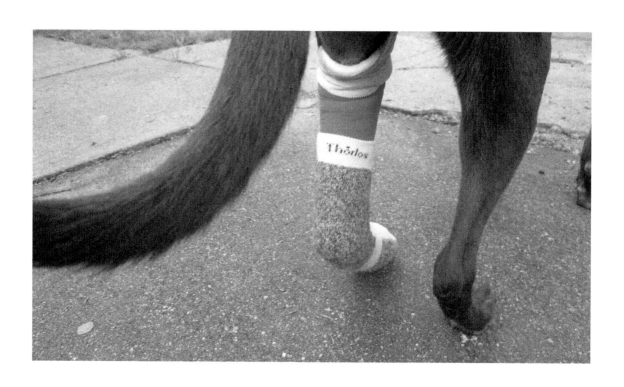

SURGERY

I'm not sure if anybody really understood how many times within the next few months we went back and forth between home and the little animal hospital and back and forth between home and the big Animal Medical Center. I know I didn't. It's not like I had anything better to do – or even that I minded the travel and the destinations. I for sure did not. And so, a few days after I saw Dr. Tamara and I was forced to wear that awful cone around my neck and head, I had yet another trip to the big 24-hour Animal Medical Center. From the time we were in the large parking lot to the time we were in the large hospital lobby, I saw lots of dogs whom I wanted to get to know and applied my energy toward that goal, but Mom yanked in the opposite direction and kept me on a short leash to prevent any contact with them. She also kept me on a short leash so that I would have to walk *s-l-o-w-l-y*: This had something to do with protecting my broken ankle bone.

Whenever I started pulling ahead, Mom said, "Joey, walk *s-l-o-w-l-y*" in an increasingly irritated voice. I ignored her and continue forging ahead. And Mom wasn't the only one who wanted me to take it easy. The doctors didn't want me putting so much weight on my rear legs because that could really hurt my broken ankle. When I would jump up on another dog at the hospital to play and make friends, Mom would snap, "Joey, off! You're going to hurt your ankle." I heard her; I just didn't obey.

Pretty soon after our arrival at the animal hospital that morning, a new doctor, Dr. Ken, came out and made friends with me. Then with little hesitation, he, Mom and I went to one of the little examining rooms, more quickly than I wanted, more *s-l-o-w-l-y* than she did.

Now the talk was *x-rays*. The light to the room was out but pictures of my toe bones, foot bones, and ankle bones were hanging right up there on the illuminated wall. Dr. Ken pointed to the illuminated wall to show Mom where my toes were broken and where my ankle was broken. He pointed to the wall to show her where he wanted to do surgery and what he wanted to do, and she was paying attention to that glowing wall. But I wasn't. The scents were overwhelming, and I pointed my head to the door, to the tiny opening where the door met the wall, to try to find a way out.

Next, the room filled with light again and Mom and the technician had me lie down on the floor while Dr. Ken took off my old splint, cleaned my wounds, wrapped my leg in bandages, made me a new splint and rebandaged the splint. This new splint was a little shorter than the old one. It made it easier for me to bend my knee but it still kept my toes and ankle immobilized so they could continue to heal. Was this ever going to end?

Mom's face suddenly broke into a big smile. "I love it!" she exclaimed ecstatically, her excitement a reference to the mango color of the outer bandages. But that's where she and I differed. I loved to see Mom smile, it made my tail wag, but her excitement about this simply did not rub off on me.

That night, back home with my parents, I was hearing my name a lot again. This time, I was also hearing the words *go* and *surgery*. I knew *go*, I didn't know *surgery*, but Mom didn't seem worried about this *surgery*. In fact, she seemed pretty happy and relaxed when she talked about *surgery*. Maybe *surgery* was a new kind of food or the name of somebody who was coming over, or a new place to discover!

Actually, this *surgery* was going to happen the day after tomorrow and I was going to stay overnight at Angell that night, and the next night, and the plan was for me to return home the following day.

What was this *surgery* and why was Mom so happy and relaxed about it? The surgery was to fix the broken bones in my ankle and she was happy about it because it might allow me to run again, just like I used to. There you had it. People were talking about me running again. I was glad Mom wasn't worried about this surgery because if she had been worried about it, I might have been worried too.

That evening, my parents made me comfortable. Once again my bed traveled: Mom went into the living room, picked up my bed, and carried it right into the kitchen so that I might spend some time with her and Dad there while they were cooking dinner. I had an early dinner and I got all my medications in before 8 p.m. At 8 p.m. my parents took away my food bowl, but I still could drink water for a few more hours. That was okay with me. I didn't have much of an appetite anyway.

The next morning began as usual: Dad and I had our private sunrise walk, along which we saw a few bunnies, whom I knew not to try to chase. That walk was not followed by my morning treat, or by another nap, however. What took place next was an unusual early morning car ride with Dad, though the car ride made me forget all about not having received my morning treat. Was Dad bringing me to work with him? Not quite. This ride ended up at the big Animal Medical Center. And once again, there were animals in every nook and cranny of the lobby, accompanied by their families, and people going to and fro.

Soon, somebody came up to us and asked, "Joey?" and this person and I went off together to the back rooms. I was so happy to make this promenade with my newest friend. I remained there in the back rooms with new people and new animal friends, and then I don't remember much after that.

A dog doesn't have a concept of surgery. But a dog definitely knows when he's feeling groggy. And groggy I felt. That evening I had a sleepover with the other dogs in this now familiar-feeling hospital. Although I was away from home, the presence of doctor friends and the other animals comforted me. One of the nice technicians took me outside for a walk in the dog park on this warm and beautiful night.

That evening, as I lay down to sleep, I had a new splint on my leg.

I started feeling like myself the next morning, for the first time in ages. To top that off, once back home, I was not confined to the living room: I was allowed to walk freely around the dining room, the living room and the kitchen on my own.

My parents had another big surprise for me: My water bowl was back in the kitchen, back in its old familiar spot in the kitchen, and I was able to drink water right in the kitchen. The familiarity of my life back home comforted me. It had also given me more hope, and more ideas.

Dad had gone downstairs into the basement, leaving the door slightly open behind him. And that's when familiarity overcame me and I made for the slightly opened door to the basement, nudged it further open with my nose, and started down the steps to the basement, my dear old basement. I loved the basement: Dad often worked down there. I also had a crate down there where I would go when I needed a sanctuary. My front paws were on the first step to the basement and I was heading down when the air cracked with the sound of "Joey, NO!"

I don't know what the big deal was, but next thing I knew the lead was attached to my collar and Mom was walking me down the stairs, on the lead, one step at a time. Might this have had something to do with The Instructions? I was too tired to mind.

I walked toward where Dad sat and sat at his feet. Mom unclipped the lead and returned upstairs. When next I saw her she was carrying my bed down the stairs into the basement, and she placed it on the floor also next to Dad's feet. I understood. It was nice to be home, nice to be able to walk up and down stairs, even with the lead attached, nice to be in the basement with my parents, nice to be anywhere with my parents, nice to be able to fall sound asleep in my own bed.

But my parents were wondering about the next thing: They were saying, "Is his experience going to stop him from trying to dig his way out again?"

And maybe you too are asking, "Has Joey learned his lesson?"

But that wasn't the question I was asking.

HISTORY LESSON

Banchory Bolo was one of the first great Labrador Retrievers. Born in 1915, he lived in Great Britain and was the first Lab who was a champion as a great hunter and a great show dog.

Born with the name of Caerhowell Bully, for the first two years of his life he moved from family to family. His owners and trainers didn't like the feisty dog who, in turn, didn't like being mistreated by them. They told everybody that Caerhowell Bully was a problem and that he was wild and stupid. Then one day Caerhowell Bully's luck turned. Lorna Countess Howe, who had become heartbroken after her dog died, showed up. She saw this dog and, though he was sick and unclean and growled when she would talk to him even in a kindly voice, decided to give him a try.

This understanding woman took the miserable dog to a caring kennel where they trained dogs to go into the fields with the hunters and to retrieve the small game; at this kennel he received a new name, Banchory Bolo. Still, the dog was wild, often running around for an hour or so before he would let anybody catch him. Would Countess Howe give up on her new Labrador? She brought her newly named Banchory Bolo out to a large field to see. He was full of energy and displayed a natural interest in the rabbits and bunnies, and the Countess was optimistic about training him. She determined that he needed at all times to be treated gently or he would be reminded of his earlier mistreatment and become out of control. And so with the dedicated Countess, he learned how to trust again, and how to behave like a champion.

One day Banchory Bolo heard a stable boy crack a whip and he became frightened: he had a flashback of the trauma of his younger days. Instantly, he ran away, jumping over a high gate that was topped with iron spikes. Seriously injuring himself, he hid for hours, until midnight. Meanwhile, back home, the Countess Howe had left the front door open for him in case he chanced to return home. Later that evening, he snuck home, bleeding from his injuries acquired while dashing from the stable, and settled into the basket that was his bed and that was set by the bed of the Countess. When she discovered him there and wounded, and these were the days before there were telephones, the Countess found a veterinarian who lived miles away and who attended to the dog, stitching him up while the dog lay still and compliant.

It was this event that set Bolo on his path to faithfulness to the Countess and trust in her caring of him. And one year later, Banchory Bolo became the first Labrador in history to earn a dual championship, a championship as both a hunter and as a show dog.

And Banchory Bolo sired Banchory Danilo, who sired Haylers Danilo, who sired Poppleton Black Lancer, who sired Poppleton Golden Major, who sired Poppleton Golden Sunray, who sired Poppleton Lieutenant, who sired Siant Pride, who sired Sandylands Shadow, who sired Sandylands Tandy, my great-great-great-grandfather, who sired Follytower Merrybrook Black Stormer, both my great-great-great-grandfather and my great-great-great-great-grandfather.

Dogs like us live in two worlds. We are dogs with the long and proud history of our breed; and we are part of a human family. Our lives and our welfare turn on the cruelty of some, and on the goodness of others. And those who share their goodness and trust with us are rewarded with unbroken loyalty and companionship.

LIGHTNING BOLT

In this world I quickly became deeply dependent upon the goodness of others. Each of the countless times I left the Animal Medical Center, I left with my leg wrapped in clean new bandages whose color my parents got all excited over. I didn't. This time, the bandage which I got after my surgery sported a yellow lightning bolt against a blue bandage, designed specifically for me. Someone at the Animal Medical Center must have thought that I liked to bolt from the back yard as fast as lightning. Of all the colors and bandages, this one was everybody's favorite.

Then there was the plastic bag. Whenever it was time to go outside, Mom or Dad put the running sock on my foot, and over the sock they then wrapped a white plastic wastebasket bag. Next they either got some tape and taped the plastic bag closed or they twisted and twisted the top and tied it into a knot so that the bag stayed on my leg. This whole operation seemed to take forever, especially because I was quivering from anticipation.

It was also difficult for me to balance myself on three legs while they were putting my foot into the sock and then again when they put my foot and leg, with its sock, into the plastic bag. But through it all, I learned one new word, *Lift*.

Once I got outside and walking, at some point somebody would come up to me, or from a distance would turn his head and follow me, and would ask and point.

"What's that?" They were pointing to my shaved leg and shaved back. It was unlike me, and also too bad, that I didn't feel like playing with others during these days.

One morning Mom took me out early for my afternoon walk. Cars were parked up and down both sides of our road and people were walking everywhere – on the road, on the sidewalks . . . We headed to the Carriage Lane where even more people were congregating, people sitting, people eating, people standing, people yelling, people laughing. The berm was thick with people and dogs having a good time. Whole families with children were cheering. People with dogs were also cheering. People with several dogs were cheering. The wide avenue where I wasn't allowed to run was teaming with people who were all running, and they were all running in the same direction, very quickly, and they were running without dogs. It was the Boston Marathon and it had come right to our neighborhood. What a walk with Mom! I didn't want to run; I just wanted to be everywhere, to see everyone, to play with every dog, and every person, and every child, all at the same time. Mom worked hard to restrain me, and she wasn't having much fun. Then she stopped in her tracks.

"Dr. Kiko! How great to see you! Joey, it's Dr. Kiko!" Dr. Kiko's grin immediately appeared, and he came over to Mom and me, though as much as I loved Dr. Kiko, I was at that point much more interested in the dogs who were there. Was I surprised to see Dr. Kiko? I had suspected that Dr. Kiko was a runner, too.

By the month of May, it had been weeks since I had been in our back yard, with its soft grass, shady bushes and trees and sun bath. But there came a day when I was allowed to enter, although still subject to the rules: I had to be wearing the sock, the plastic bag had to go over that, and I had to be on the leash at all times. "Joey might want to chase a squirrel or run to say hello to a neighbor and the leash will prevent him from running off," my surgeon had told my parents. So down the three steps and to the garden I went, with sock and plastic bag, and lead. I felt awkward, but I was outside. Mom walked around a bit, holding onto the lead, and I walked around a little bit, by her side. She walked to our hammock and lay down in its webbing, the rays of the sunlight shining on her face, and I lay down on the blue grass by her side. Then still holding onto the lead, Mom closed her eyes and sighed. I closed my eyes, pointed my face toward the sun, or into the breeze. And sighed.

The sun was high above the trees, everything beneath it being warmed and nourished.

From where I lay in the back yard, I noticed the hole over on the side that I had dug for my escape. It was still there. But on this day I was not getting any ideas.

Another outdoor place where Mom now allowed me to go during the day was onto the deck, way high up, on my parents' second floor. Here I could be outside and stand beneath the bright sky as it covered me with its warmth, and I didn't have to be on the lead. This is the place where Mom had stood in the morning light twelve weeks earlier when she noticed that I wasn't sunbathing beside the apple tree or resting under the apple tree. This is the place where she had stood when she noticed that I was on "the other side" side of the fence.

As gradually as the days were warming up, every now and then when I walked I was using my fourth paw, putting my fourth leg down. Maybe now, as my surgeon Dr. Ken said, my muscles would get nice and strong again.

But it wasn't all perfect. I couldn't play my favorite game, tennis ball, with other people or by myself. I wasn't allowed to hurt my ankle, which was in the splint and was trying to heal from the surgery. I also wasn't in the mood to play tennis ball.

The closest I could come to playing tennis ball was watching ball games on the television, which held my interest for a few moments but not much longer. I was watching ball games with my parents so that we could spend time together. I could choose to watch TV or go to sleep, and I would do the former until it bored me, and then I would do the latter.

As the days slipped by, Mom and Rosie's mom continued communicating, waiting for the day when my doctors would say that I was well enough to walk for longer distances and to be around other dogs. Mom would come and give me the report. "Joey, I talked to Rosie's mom today and just as soon as you're able to, we'll get together with Rosie and take a nice walk."

The name Rosie didn't strike a familiar chord. But the anticipation of a walk was a bit of a tease. Mom would say this and then we'd remain indoors, where we were.

And when, Mom, do you expect this walk to take place?

Meanwhile, it was time for me to celebrate one week since the surgery to repair my broken ankle, and to celebrate a return to normalcy, and it was also time for my parents to begin thinking more about my escaping again. This is how it happened:

I had been in the sun porch, an enclosed room that connects the kitchen with the outside back yard, and Mom had been in the sun porch with me. Then Mom went outside, opened the gate to the driveway, went out to the driveway, and came back in to the sun porch with me. Then she went inside the house to the kitchen. I carefully observed that she had left the sun porch door open and that she had also left the gate to the driveway open. While Mom wasn't looking at me, I turned away and walked down the three steps that lead to the outside and walked through the gate and out onto the driveway. I think I did this all very well, I thought I had timed it very well, but that is when she saw me – and what I was up to.

"Joey, no!" rang out, clearly coming from one direction. "Come inside." She had me. I turned around toward that direction and looked back at Mom as if to say, "What's the problem?" but I came inside anyway, though regretfully.

I had picked one moment when she was distracted. To me, there had been an opportunity and I had seized it.

Thus my parents began thinking about my future and what to do in order to prevent me from getting out of the yard again, unattended. They began talking to people and dog-owners about what to do to keep me from escaping again. My parents had all sorts of ideas, none of them, from my point of view, good ideas.

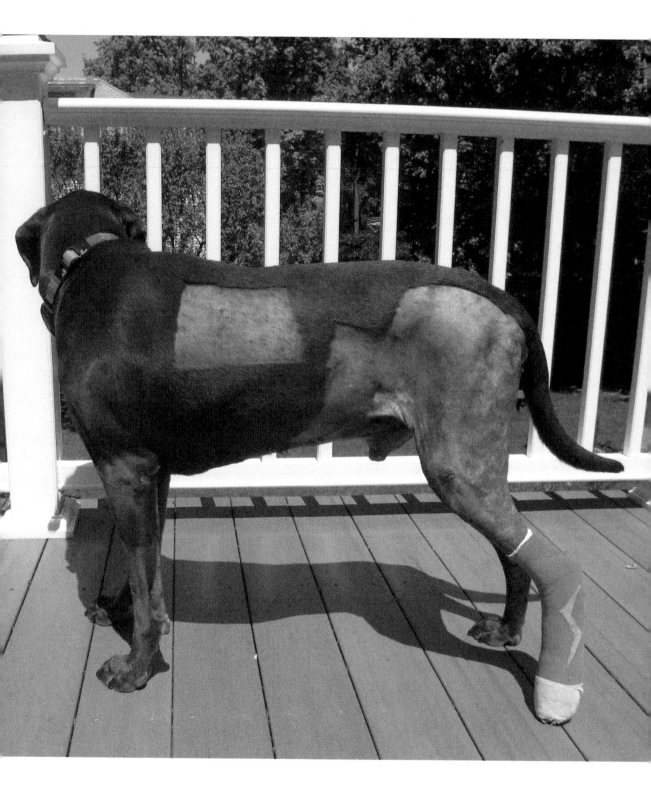

Even Mary, my favorite mail carrier with her pocketful of treats, put her two cents in. "How are you going to keep Joey in?" she asked Mom. "They're diggers. They dig. Digging is what they do." Sure, I loved Mary. But sometimes she talked a bit too much.

And yet, with each new day, I still celebrated that my leg was healing more and more. My belly was mostly healed, though I had some scars there, and the undercoat of my rear leg and back was starting to grow back in. Less and less often the people who passed me by would stop and ask, "What happened to him?" More and more often I felt increased energy. But I still needed a lot of rest. I spent a lot of the day sleeping, which was important, because my bones and ligaments needed to heal. Besides, where was I going to go? What else was I going to do?

Because I was now allowed to go out to the back yard just to rest and without the lead on me at all times, I gradually became much more relaxed. Being a part of nature's annual rebirth soothed and consoled me. I was also encouraged by the increasing number of children in our neighborhood who would pass by our home and stop to call out, over the fence, "Hi, Joey" when they saw me.

Mom, however, still didn't want me to get too excited. So I had to make the most of the good times when Mom would take me out for a relaxed walk and the neighborhood children would congregate around me and say, "Can I pet him?"

"Sit," Mom would command me, and I would sit and then Mom would allow the neighborhood children to come over to pet me, one child at a time, one pet at a time. It was these moments that sustained me.

Eating well continued to be a big focus of my parents' attention. At the same time, one thing I didn't like was eating dog food.

I could go a whole day without eating. Even in the good old days when Dad and I used to take runs for as long as one hour, I still would come home and not eat. Dad would go to work in the morning and come home at night, and my food bowl would still be full from breakfast. Sometimes I wasn't even interested in drinking water.

During these healing months, my parents were making a big deal out of my eating two meals each day. Mom's and my stare-down contests increased. I had to take medications that had to be taken after a meal but I was now disinterested in the chicken broth. I stared Mom down so she wouldn't make me eat, and she stared me down until I *would* eat. During these staring contests, I wanted her to understand that my eating that breakfast was the worst thing that could possibly happen to me. Why couldn't I get some of that good food that she and Dad were eating? Would I wake up one day and find their foods in my bowl, where kibble once was? Would I ever wake up to find that I could go to the backyard by myself and unattended?

Within a minute or two, she would be staring me down, and I would be eating. In fact, I would eat my entire bowl of breakfast. She would win.

Then she would say, "Good boy! Good boy, Joey!" and give me my medication.

After that, I would get a treat. Eating my treat made me forget about all my other woes.

WHO IS WISE?

It is written: "Who is wise? He who learns from everybody." Does that include learning from dogs? We soon would find out.

The days stretched out, each one arriving earlier and staying later, and the sun's rays revealed corners and furrows that had lain obscured in winter's and spring's shadows. The ground softened up once more. The leaves on the trees became so thick that in places they blocked the sunlight from reaching the ground.

My bed was in the living room, behind the barricade, light beginning to brighten the room, when Dad came down the stairs each morning, all prepared to go running; I still eyed him with a longing to be out running with him. And although the seasons were changing, Dad continued to be adamant: "No, Joey. Not this time," he said, then passed before my eyes on his way out the front door.

Along those solitary runs of Dad's, other runners would now ask him, "Where's your dog?" or "Is your dog okay?"

Late one morning while Dad, Mom and I were together in the kitchen, Dad spoke to Mom, as he often did, as if I weren't even there: "Guess what happened to me this morning while I was out running. One walker who doesn't even have a dog said to me, 'Isn't Joey your dog? Watching Joey run with such abandon and having so much fun is such an inspiration to me.' And then she said, 'Seeing Joey run makes me want to walk every day.'" Dad surely was so proud of me, and at that moment he was happy, but he was a little sad too. The words must have had special meaning, however, because after breakfast with Mom he proudly took me for my morning walk around the block.

And so it seemed that even though my neighborhood hadn't seen me run in months, even though running still seemed to be a long way off and I was still limited to my one walk around the block twice a day, my place on the Carriage Lane was reserved.

And I continued to get better.

Getting better didn't always involve a lot of activity. It often seemed like I wasn't doing much of anything. I spent long hours asleep or half asleep. Sometimes Mom would go out and when she came home, I was in the same place as where I'd been when she'd left. So was my food bowl. Mom would walk into the kitchen and say, "Hey, Joey. Anything exciting happen while I was out?" and she would laugh. She thought that was funny.

Often, when my parents were home, they were looking at me. It wasn't because they wanted to play with me. They were looking at me and examining me. They were also often talking to each other in low, quiet voices as they did this. Very often they were looking at my injured paw at the bottom of the splint where it was open to the air to make sure that my toes looked healthy and that the pads of my feet were not swollen. They had learned to look at my bandages and at the bottom of my splint to make sure I wasn't chewing at them. They had learned to look at my bandages to see that they remained dry.

Lack of privacy continued to be an issue with me. I never really had much privacy in our home, especially because I often preferred to be around my family, and if I did want privacy I could go to my crate in the basement. But now people were looking at me all the time. One evening, Mom noticed me standing on three legs and paws and holding my fourth leg up in the air. She assumed this was part of the healing process. She was wrong. I was holding my leg up in the air because it hurt and it hurt because the bandages were too tight.

The next day, she was looking at me again and noticed that I was licking my bandages. This time, she repeated Dr. Tamara's words, "What's he trying to tell us?" I didn't offer any ideas or suggestions, unless you consider my looking at her with my big wide open brown eyes a suggestion.

Once again to the telephone she headed. "The sock – just put it on and if he continues licking his bandages, then take him to the emergency room," she heard. So Mom put Dad's running sock on and left it on throughout the night, while we all went to sleep.

The next evening, except for the sounds of Mom *tap tap* tapping at her little machine, and the refrigerator running, all was quiet in our home. I was lying in my bed in the corner of the dining room. Mom was in the little front office, within sight, minding her own business. Dad was upstairs. I was minding my own business, just slowly chipping away at my splint, when Mom suddenly turned around to face me and gave me the eye, at which point I paused in my effort, rolled my eyes up to meet hers, and froze. Silently, she walked over to me, crouched down at my level, looked at my injured leg and noticed my bandages were wet. The silent treatment continued while she eyed me up and down. Up and down. Up and down I followed her movements. Then I heard it.

"Phil! Come right away!" Dad appeared in a flash. He knelt at my side, Mom knelt at my side and Dad declared, "The bandage is on too tight."

Good! It was really exciting for me when Dad got my sock and put it back on my foot and got the plastic bag because I recognized those as signs that I was going outside! And was I ever correct. With a wag of my tail, I forgot all about my aching paw and within a few more minutes Dad and I were in the car and on the road. Life could still hold delightful surprises!

The big 24-hour Animal Medical Center was – once again – our next stop. For once there weren't so many other animals in the lobby. The emergency care doctor immediately came out to the lobby to see me and right there in the hospital lobby saw that my bandages were too tight. From the front desk she quickly obtained a pair of scissors and cut my bandages open right there! *Relief!* Then she took me with her into an examination room, took off the old bandages and re-bandaged my splint.

"Will there never be an end to these visits to the Animal Medical Center?" Mom moaned, scratched her head, and exhaled.

I hoped not. But at the same time I was standing with all four paws on the ground and mostly walking with all four legs.

Three weeks had now gone by since my ankle surgery, and one full month had gone by since I was hit by the car. Barely had a few days passed since my last excursion to the hospital when Mom again noticed that I had eaten off the bottoms of the bandages and that I had chewed away at my splint. I heard a mix of exasperation – and concern – in her voice. But again, within ten minutes of her noticing that, the plastic bag was back on my foot, we were back in the car, my boredom had vanished, my joy at the pleasure of a car ride had renewed my spirit, and I had forgotten about my annoying splint and bandages. In no time, I was at the Animal Medical Center and among my canine friends once again.

I met so many children there. One child was Wanda, who was there with her sister Miri because her hamster Cookie Dough had been playing with her sister's' hamster and Cookie Dough had fallen and was badly hurt. I met another child who looked at my tail, which was more and more rapidly waving back and forth with each new moment and each new giggle of his, and asked, "Why is his tail doing that?"

"It's called wagging," Mom answered. "He's wagging his tail to express happiness."

Later, Wanda again came by and this time with tearful eyes and holding a little box in her hands, said that inside the box was Cookie Dough and that the good doctors couldn't save his life. I gave the brave Wanda kisses and Mom gave her a little hug and said, "Goodbye, Cookie Dough." Then we watched Wanda and Miri and their mom softly walk out of the hospital, Mom and I looking on, silently.

It was particularly easy to meet other dogs here because the hospital had an entire 'Dogs' waiting room! Here, I met many dogs who were terrified of being in the hospital and who were clinging so tightly to their parents' legs or hiding under their parents' coats. I tried to make friends with these dogs, extending the flexi-lead as far as it would go, but they would retreat further into any dark shadows they could find. And anyway that's when Mom would call or pull me back, saying, "Joey, no. He doesn't want to play with you. Leave him alone."

I also saw many courageous, spirited and proud dogs. One had three legs and was hopping as quickly as I was walking. Another had an injury to his hind legs and was using his strong front legs to pull himself forward.

But as happy as I was while in the reception hall, soon it was time to go into one of the little examination rooms. There my new doctor gave me two new 'toys'. The first was a new little bag to replace the plastic trash bag. This *protective boot* slipped on over my sock and closed easily. The second 'toy' was a new collar, an even larger collar, to make sure that I didn't continue to chew at my bandages and splint. Was there no limit to the size of these things? Was there no limit to how miserable I could feel? Fortunately, I was allowed to take the car ride home without this misery encircling my neck and head.

And that's when Mom and Dad showed their ability to learn, once again, for as soon as I was back home in my bed and sanctuary in the living room, even before Mom could put the new collar on me, I had started chewing on my new bandage. In a minute, she had the new and larger collar on me, and there it firmly remained for the rest of the evening.

One night, when I was feeling better and more energetic, Dad asked Mom, "When is he getting his next set of x-rays taken?" We still had room to hope.

For every rule that was soon relaxed, another took its place. For every one thing that my parents had succeeded in accomplishing regarding me, a new challenge took its place. Let's take jumping up onto the sofas, every dog's delight, of which we had three in our home. My parents had a rule that I was not allowed onto the sofas because they figured if I was allowed onto the sofa, I would also think that I was allowed onto the bed, which was forbidden. Now I wasn't allowed on the sofas, doctor's orders.

All of our sofas were on the ground floor, two of them perfectly situated right by windows, and all were within my side of the barricade. It was a perfect setup. Naturally, when I was confined to within the wooden gate, the sofa challenge was on. For a while, Mom lay a broom on one sofa, and that was supposed to keep me off. It worked for a while, but we didn't have enough brooms for all the sofas.

One day Mom came home with a small, round, shiny and mysterious object. She placed the odd object on the sofa. "Aha," her eyes declared, as she looked at me and snickered. She tested it out. "Joey, come" she said, and patted the sofa cushion on which this new object rested. I was interested in this object and allured by the invitation to be on the sofa. When I jumped up onto the sofa and made the cushions move, the little odd object emanated a high, loud, and shrill *buzzzz* and I jumped off, frightened by the noise. "Perfect," Mom gloated. And there she left this object, and there the object remained, when she went out.

Her ploy worked for a while, and then I reasoned to jump up onto the side of the sofa where the buzzer was not. That worked, until the day when my Mom came home and when she walked in the front door and heard a big *thud*.

Now the first things she's always going to do are to look at my eyes and to see what I'm thinking.

Okay, Mom. So you heard a big thud. And I look guilty: I'm walking slowly toward you and low to the ground, nose just about touching it. But what if I hadn't been on the sofa? What if that big thud was just my big clunky splint hitting the floor as I got off of my low bed to stand up and greet you? What if I just look guilty because you'll never believe me anyway?

But with all the restrictions, I didn't fully appreciate how fortunate I was until this too changed. Though my parents will never know the truth, the rules for leaving me home alone soon changed, again. Now, when I was home alone, no longer was I confined to the living room.

Rather, everything was now reversed. From now on when Mom left home, she made sure that I was *outside* of the living room with the dog gate to the living room closed so that I couldn't get *into* the living room.

To make it even more impossible for me to live a normal life, she made sure the door to the basement remained closed. Then, to prevent me from going up the stairs to the second floor, she put another dog gate at the base of that staircase. These left me access only the kitchen and the dining room, which is where I now spent all my miserable and lonely hours when I was home alone. The advantage was that the shades and curtains no longer had to be drawn and the rooms no longer had to be darkened. The light of day was again my companion.

But of course to make matters worse, the day after the big *thud*, Mom and Dad put the extra-large Elizabethan collar on me just before they went out. *No problem*, they thought. *We'll have a miserable dog, but he won't chew at his splint.* They were right about having a miserable dog, but wrong about my not chewing at my splint and bandages. A little while later, when my parents came home, Mom noticed my bandages were wet and my splint had been chewed at.

I had managed to chew at the bottom of my splint, even with the large sized collar.

I wasn't saying anything, but Mom started talking about when my next bandage change was going to be. And her frustration was accumulating.

June eventually became July and my parents were counting the weeks and days until it was time for salvation and my second set of x-rays. Maybe the doctors would decide to remove my splint. Maybe then I would be able to run with Dad in the morning before the sunlight appeared. Maybe I would be able to take a walk with my sister and littermate, Rosie. Everybody hoped. But nobody knew for sure.

And then it happened.

In the examination room of the large hospital, I was lying on the floor with one doctor and Mom holding me and comforting me, while another doctor, Dr. Cara, cut off my old bandages and removed the splint, washed my paw and leg, examined my foot and leg and put antiseptic cream on my sores. Occasionally I felt uncomfortable and shook my leg a little but then I would hear "Good boy" and Mom would pet me and pretty soon I was calm again. For the most part, this was boring, and I almost fell asleep, I think. The two doctors and Mom kept on talking, sometimes about how the sore on my leg was looking better. Soon, my paw was wrapped in fluffy soft white bandages and then a red bandage layered on top. But no splint.

The splint was off. I immediately felt the difference. Furthermore, the splint was going to remain off. Right before leaving the examining room, Mom directed me to "Say 'Thank you' to Dr. Cara" and I went to Dr. Cara and gave her a kiss. She handed me a treat and I, being properly raised, had the good manners of taking and eating. I then snapped up the other treat she handed me.

"He loves me because I give him treats," the doctor said.

"No," Mom answered. "He loves you because he loves you." *That's right, Mom. Tell them something about puppy love!*

Home again, I found myself with nothing to do and nobody to pay much attention to me. If I was frustrated, I had no way to express it. The afternoon, as many before it, dragged on and on. It was a huge letdown from the excitement – and attention – of the morning. Even when Mom was home, she wasn't paying any attention to me. I was living in an afternoon without purpose.

As the day wore on and on and I managed to make myself comfortable by Mom's side, the telephone rang. Mom started talking. She turned to me and said, "Joey, we're going to go out." By her tone this didn't sound like a trip to the Animal Hospital, but for so many months, where else had we ever gone?

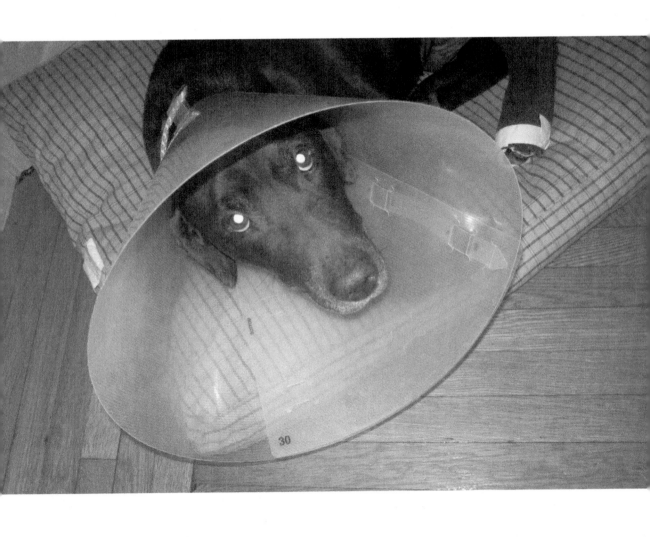

She put the sock on my foot, the bootie over that, and clipped the lead on me. We walked to her car, she gave me a boost and I took my seat in the back. Out of the driveway we turned in the other direction, away from the little animal hospital and away from the large Animal Medical Center and toward The Woods where I liked to go by myself when Mom wasn't around. Then we passed The Woods. After driving for a while through streets that became more and more crowded with people and automobiles, she pulled the car up to a curb and there stood a surprise I had definitely not expected. Dad! He opened the car door to the back seat, I got out – and Mom drove away. Some new Animal Hospital I didn't know about? Dad and I waited on the busy sidewalk until Mom appeared on foot. Then the three of us walked along a tiny narrow alley to a new building, went up the elevator, and the doors closed. What was I supposed to do here? Soon the elevator doors opened and we entered a whole new place, a place where there were no animals. What was I supposed to do now?

"Joey!" People came from everywhere called to me, a certain occasion for some vigorous tail wagging. Then more and more people arrived. "Joey! It's Joey!" I didn't know them but they knew me. People got an especially big kick out of my sock. This was indeed a special day: It was national "Take Your Dog to Work Day" and I was, after all, a working dog.

Then we all walked to a little room which was Dad's office.

Being quiet and sitting became an almost impossible task because more and new people kept showing up and wanting to pet me, wanting me to play with them and have their photographs taken with me. Mom took a lot of photographs and, like usual, she kept saying, "Joey, stick your tongue back in your mouth." But I didn't obey her.

When Mom said, "Joey, sit," everybody in unison would screech, "He's so gooooood!" and then I would get excited and stand up. Mom wasn't so happy about that because I still had my injured foot and she didn't want me standing up too much. But a dog has to take advantage of the opportunity to make all the friends he can.

Dad's little room looked a lot like home because it had books and things everywhere, including on the floor. Dad brought me a bowl of water and Mom said, "Joey, drink." I *really* felt right at home. People were watching me drink and they said with adoration, "Wow! He's so good!" I felt happy, if not a bit overwhelmed, which in turn increased my thirst.

The bald patches on my fur were also very popular. Although my coat was beginning to grow back, these people also pointed and asked, "What's that?" and Dad was explaining and explaining, which seemed to make him very happy, and everybody pointed a lot to my back and I understood that I had to "stay" while they were going through this.

Dad went back to his desk to work. To a Retriever, *working* means running, saving lives, rescuing injured people, herding fish, herding sheep, retrieving dinner, helping people cross streets, and maybe digging a nice hole in the ground. But to Dad *work* meant that I was supposed to be quiet and *sit* and *stay*. This wasn't productive work, as far as I could determine.

Yet with every "Take Your Dog to Work Day" there also follows a 'Take Your Dog Back Home' moment.

As wonderful as it was to spend time with Dad at Dad's office in the middle of the day and make new friends there, to walk through the tiny back alleys of a new place with new smells, sounds and sights, it was also time for Mom and me to leave. So out of Dad's office and down the hall we all walked, as everybody called out, "Bye, Joey!" Into the elevator Mom and I stepped, I without my splint and with my unceasingly wagging tail speaking for me.

With the splint off and my place in the world of people and places again available to me, I was so relieved: I was ready to run a mile.

Except that when I returned home that afternoon, I still was not allowed to walk more than a block in either direction.

There were so many times during this long ordeal in which my hopes rose like a squirrel fleeing up a tree to get away from me, and then sank like a rock. In fact, my parents were still keeping me on my short lead whenever we were outside and I was still on the lead when we would go up and down the stairs. But at least, I suppose, I was allowed to climb the steps and go upstairs, or downstairs.

With the splint removed, in some ways I was now more limited. With less support for my injured leg, I had to be more careful than I'd had to be recently. With the splint, I'd been ascending and descending the stairs numerous times a day. Now my parents only let me upstairs once – to go to bed for the night, my bed having been moved upstairs once again – and downstairs once – to go out in the morning for my morning walk with Dad. I also had to stay downstairs all day, excluded from the living room, until bedtime, when I was allowed back upstairs. The rules kept changing and changing.

Once Dad would bring me downstairs with him each morning, I still didn't enjoy watching him leave home to go running without me and watching him return home from his run all by himself.

Still, although my leg was still bandaged, without the splint I felt lighter and happier, my leg was getting more air and there was less irritation. My mood noticeably improved. People who looked at my leg still saw the bandages. They couldn't tell that the splint was not there under the bandages. But I could.

Fortunately, I still was brought to the large Animal Medical Center each week for checkups. The visits also meant a continuation of the usual questions by spectators. The most popular question was "What happened to him?" while people stared at me, expecting me to stand still or sit still while Mom launched into her explanation and other dogs passed by without my being permitted to play with them.

Two children came over to pet me on one of those visits and then pointed to their two dogs and said, "Our dog has a broken ankle too and he has plates and screws in his leg too."

Mom was of course wondering, "But does he run?"

If their dog could have talked to me he might have said, "Don't worry. Just like me, you will be able to run again." But dogs don't communicate that way. And who could see that far into the future?

I dwelled somewhere between either believing that I would be able to run again with Dad or wanting to believe it. The worst part of each day was when Dad left early – without me – on his running adventure.

Nighttime had taken on a new ritual. Mom, sitting silently on her sofa in the living room, would read book after book. She wanted to learn about dogs, and she wanted to learn about me.

One afternoon she started using hand signals around me.

"Stay," she said, as her open palm appeared in front of my face. "Sit," she commanded, as her open hand motioned down to the ground. Over and over again she did these hand signals every time she had a verbal command for me. When she said, "Come," she cupped her fingers together and moved them toward her in a sort of wave motion.

I took to these hand signals much more quickly than Mom probably expected. I enjoyed looking for a sign. Mom had finally become part of a grand Labrador tradition. Working Retrievers learn to obey hand signals from their handlers when they are in the field on a hunt: The silent hand signals do not betray the presence of a dog to the birds and fowl. The handler raises his arm in the air and indicates to the left, to the right, or straight ahead, and a good dog obeys. So naturally, now that Mom knew all about me, she also was going to act like a professional. I learned to listen to her and follow her hand for direction. I could see the palm of her hand telling me what to do long after her voice had quieted. She used the hand signal all by itself when Dad was asleep, and I knew just what she wanted from me, and we never disturbed Dad. I became very proud of my new skill.

And that's when people started saying, more and more, "He looks very intelligent" or "He's so obedient," although frankly they were talking way over my head.

Going up and down the stairs was another way in which I became more obedient. Most of the time when Mom walked to the stairway, I would get up and go too, even without being asked. And then she either put the lead on me or held onto my collar as I ascended or descended alongside her. At the top or the bottom, she would turn to me and say, "Joey, stay" or "Joey, sit" and use her hand signal and I would look at her and listen to her. I would sit and stay at the head of the stairs, or at the bottom, whichever it was. She would walk into some room, and then a few minutes later she'd be back – and I would still be sitting where she had left me.

Mom was happy that I was obeying her for another reason: She was hoping that this meant that I would not try to escape from our yard.

The back yard became a recreational area and an area of keen observation. Mom watched me almost as carefully as I watched her. She noticed that I wasn't going near my old digging spot. I noticed that she noticed that I walked the perimeter of our garden, walking behind the trees and bushes, sniffing everywhere, but not stopping anywhere along it to dig. When I started to dig too close to the perimeter of our yard, she noticed that as well. I noticed that she noticed that I seemed to be interested in the gate, but that I didn't linger there for long. I also noticed that she noticed that I had one spot where I was digging and that spot was near a tree near our home. She wasn't worried about this anymore. She learned that she had other things and other digging spots to worry about more.

Mom became suspicious again. She was wondering, "Would Joey behave differently if I weren't looking?" While I sat in the yard one sunny day contemplating the comforting feeling of the intensifying warmth of the season, Mom contemplated too. But she contemplated, "Will his good and obedient behavior end in a few months after he's all better?"

When Dad took me out for my early morning walk and everything glowed a soft pink, there was a renewal of my interest in the squirrels, bunnies and other dogs that didn't go without Dad's notice. All over again he warned me, "No chasing bunnies." He was telling me what I could not do, but I was hearing those old familiar warnings again, and loving it. I was also seeking out other dogs when I went outside now and was following the trails of their scents.

But what could I do with my bundled energy every day when I wasn't allowed to run or swim or stay by myself outside? When I looked at Dad, I didn't want to hear, "Joey, not today. Go back to bed." All I wanted to hear him whisper, "Come on, Joey. Let's go."

FUSION

Years of waking up at 4 a.m. with Dad had trained me to be ready for anything at any time; although that morning nobody put my breakfast in my bowl, Dad didn't leave home to go to work, my parents got me into the car and we all drove off while it was still dark out, I didn't question anything. We were having a wonderful family day, as far as I was concerned.

Our family outing ended up at our now familiar place – the big Animal Medical Center – where things again started out like usual. We stood in the 'Check in' line, where I met a dog who had eaten a corn cob. Then my parents and I went to the 'Dogs' section of the waiting room, and they sat down while I did my best to find a playmate, though there were few dogs there this time.

Soon, Dr. Dee came out and met my parents and asked, "Does he need to be knocked out so he can sit still while the x-rays are being taken?" What a crazy question. My parents said that I didn't need to be knocked out, and Mom gave the doctor a short lesson.

"Don't say 'Good dog' to him because if you say that, he will probably start wagging his tail and kissing you and then you won't be able to get the x-rays you want."

And off I headed, along with my new doctor and friend, to the radiology room.

It had been ninety-six days – thirteen weeks and five days – since I had gone running. It had been ninety-five days – thirteen weeks and four days – since I'd been injured. Ninety-five days since I'd made my decision to explore the world, on my own. Ninety-five days since I'd been allowed to walk on my own four feet.

I'm not sure what the doctor found so interesting on the x-rays but as if by some miracle on this day I was allowed to remain bare-legged and allowed to stand upright with my four feet planted on the ground. I was a little wobbly and unsteady – but I was indeed walking on all four legs.

I followed Dr. Dee back to where my parents were waiting, and we then all went into a small room that was darkened except for one wall that was lit up like the moon. In this little room the three others talked and talked and talked and looked at some glowing pictures of my bones that were shining from the glowing wall – just like my parents had done with Dr. Kiko eleven weeks earlier, just like Mom had done with Dr. Ken. They talked "broken toes" and "new bone mass" and "bones healing" and "bones fusing together" while I stood alone in the middle of the room, oblivious of them and they of me and happy to be free and standing on my four legs without any help from anyone or anything.

Soon the whole room was full of light again. I, at that moment, wasn't quite sure what to do. Here I was, a full-grown adult dog, son of a champion, grandson of champions, famed for speed, endurance, and strength, standing on all four legs but feeling awkward and wondering what to do with myself.

Three legs were strong and steady and one leg was weak and shaky. The paws of three legs were tough and firm and the paws of my fourth leg were tender and sore. *Do I allow the back of my unsteady foot to support my weight? What if the ankle of my injured hind foot is not bending like the ankle of my other hind foot?* I raised my eyes to Mom for an answer, and she was no help at all, then looked back down at my feet again. She then crouched down to my eye-level and, lowering herself to the floor, started looking at my paws and my foot from very close up, almost like she had done the morning I sat by the chain-link fence, almost like she had done the time she came to visit me in my pen in the Critical Care Unit after I was hit by the car. My injured foot felt different from the other rear foot. She looked – but she didn't touch.

And then, like always, Mom asked questions and, like always, the doctors started up again with their rules. Soon, everybody – but me – was shaking hands, smiling, and saying and doing all sorts of happy stuff. In the excitement they had forgotten all about me, which was also fine with me.

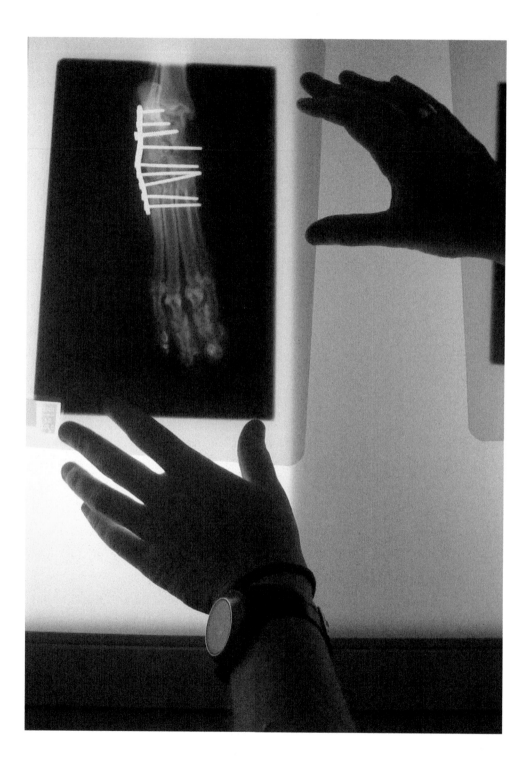

Then the door of the examination room opened. Dad attached the lead back to my collar and started to walk out the door. I followed. The floors were very slippery. The muscles of my three feet and legs carried me confidently but the muscles of my fourth foot and leg moved awkwardly. I was anxious to move quickly, but I felt very wobbly. I was slipping and sliding on the hospital floor every time I stepped on my fourth and injured leg. Yet I carried forth and kept up with Dad.

Dad continued to direct me down the long hallway and into the large, open, and sun-filled hospital lobby, past the two children waiting for the doctor to bring them back their dog who had eaten a corn cob, past the 'Dogs' waiting room off to one side along the large and open picture window and past the 'Cats' waiting room off to the other. We walked past everything and everyone, past their smiling faces and nodding heads. We walked toward the large glass doors of the hospital that separated it from the beckoning outdoors and the beginning of the rest of my life, doors that at times were an entrance and that at other times were an exit.

The large glass doors of the hospital automatically opened and an intense splash of sunshine greeted us. Dad and I weren't running – yet – but we were walking, together, all six legs of us. Mom was close behind.

WALK

The word *walk* is definitely in the top ten of any dog's vocabulary list and no sooner had we arrived home on this warm sunny afternoon when I heard the word that stood my ears on end.

"Let's take Joey for a walk" is what they actually said but the key word, the word any dog is listening for, was *walk*. The sound of my name, *Joey*, ensured my attention. First my tail started wagging left, right, left, right, with renewed power, then left, right, left, right, left, right, even more quickly and powerfully, keeping my eyes steady on my parents as much as possible. I soon started revolving in familiar circles and larger circles around my parents. Mom and Dad fulfilled my hopes: Dad got the little poop bags, another good sign, Mom got the lead, attached it to my collar, and opened the front door. There was no hesitation on my part; out we all went into the expanse of our neighborhood. There was a spirit of revelry right in front of our home as runners passed and stopped to greet me.

Mom and Dad and I then turned toward the Carriage Lane where I had been hit by the car, an event which I had long forgotten. My parents guided me to the wide grassy berm that paralleled the Carriage Lane, as it gave me something soft to walk on while my foot was still tender. Many people and dogs were promenading, some up the hill, others down the hill. Others were running alone or in groups of runners. Having picked up the scent of another dog, which is where my interest lay, I began moving quickly along the grass. My sense of urgency was balanced out by the tugging of the lead telling me to slow down, as Dad wanted to keep me at a slow pace. The summer grass felt firm under my uncertain legs. We walked one more long block. Dad now was echoing my sentiments when he said, "We can go a little further" and "He's doing fine."

I was sometimes stumbling but I *was* overall doing fine. Though my legs were uncertain, my resolve was not. My focus on the trail of scents was intense and overrode whatever it was my parents were saying about me. Joey this. Joey that.

It overrode Dad saying, "He's got to learn to walk again with that leg."

I wasn't even bothered when Mom said, "We shouldn't overdo it on the first day." I was perfectly happy to overdo it, and I continued to pull, tug, and sniff with pure delight and a new sense of urgency. Then both Mom and Dad seemed to speak with a uniform voice:

"That's enough."

We turned around to head toward home. My eager nose remained almost dusting the ground, captivated by the fresh scents and the stories they told.

Once back home, I headed straight for my water bowl, drank a full bowl of water, turned my attention to my food bowl, ate a full bowl of food and then fell, exhausted and contented, onto my bed.

I had had a short walk. I had been on the lead. But I felt free and feeling much more like myself again. That night I didn't have any thoughts of running; I was satisfied.

The next day outdid even that one. It too was sunny and I spent a lot of time with Mom outside in our garden. She had her camera bug thing so I had to do a lot of sitting and staying, but I was happy.

That evening, instead of my normal kibble, my parents unexpectedly gave some of my favorite foods, baked potatoes cut up into small cubes, without my even asking for them. As the evening wore on and we all went downstairs into the basement – myself on my own four legs and with no lead attached – and they started to make music. I love music and music makes me want to dance and howl. So when they started singing "Happy Birthday to you Happy Birthday Dear Joey Happy Birthday to you," and clapping quickly, I of course jumped up onto my hind legs and began to howl with delight. Mom stood up from the sofa she'd been sitting on and, holding my front paws, danced with me until I lost my balance, all the while Dad was saying, "Joey! Watch that tail!" And at the end of the song, together they cheered, "Jo-ey" then "Yaaaaaay!" and they sang the song once more.

I was ten years old and my parents really knew how to celebrate.

BIRD-WATCHING

Now that I no longer had bandages on my leg, life was moving rapidly toward the familiar – and I did everything I could to move rapidly with it.

One week after my bandages were removed and my wounds had time to dry out, I suffered with my first bathing in almost four months. I had always disliked standing awkwardly in the shower and this time was no different, though I didn't resist Mom when she, holding a pile of towels, waved me over to the shower. I disliked having water poured all over me, though I allowed Mom to do it. I disliked being all lathered up, though I allowed Mom to do that too. I also disliked standing there doing nothing for five minutes, all wet and lathered up. And I disliked when the water again came and dripped all over me, though I allowed Mom to do that, too. I *liked* when Mom said, "Joey, all done. You're clean! Good boy!" and dried me off with the towel, but I preferred the dog's way of drying off – dragging and rubbing my body along the floor and the carpets and the side of the bed, and anything soft I could find. I also came to understand that after each shower, Mom was going to blow warm air on my ears, head, neck and chest with the small dryer that she held in her hands, and maybe this made it all worth it. "How does that feel, Joey? Good?" As warm air from the drier massaged my muscles, I could have stood there all day. And that's when Mom attached the lead to my collar and downstairs and outside to the back yard and the welcome of the afternoon warmth we went. She then detached the lead from my collar and I found my own spot in the center of the lawn, sunlight all around me.

Our home is home to several families. Every summer a whole family of birds makes its home on the top of one of our room air conditioners, which juts out from the rear wall of our home. Seemingly endlessly, during the daylight hours Mother Bird will fly away, then come home with some food or another little piece of building material, then Father Bird will fly away, then fly home with some food or another little piece of building material, and on and on they go, taking turns, tweeting and singing as they work, coming and going, coming and going, until evening settles them down, and they quiet down, as a family. Then one day they all fly away.

And so, on this beautiful day I sat freely out in our back yard, as close to motionless as I could get, and heard and watched the busy family raising its children to one day fly away. For a long time after that, I just closed my eyes and snoozed.

My parents, meanwhile, were watching me like hawks to see when it was okay for Dad and me to go running again.

A series of long daytime neighborhood walks with Mom began, with us walking at the same quick pace. She wanted to strengthen my injured leg and build up my endurance. She was looking to see if I was limping or using three legs and holding my injured leg up when I moved quickly. She was looking to see if I was walking on the grass, on the asphalt, or on the sidewalk. She was looking to see if the pads of my paws were tender or were getting calloused and tough. She was looking at everything. There was no avoiding her gaze.

One day, my parents and I were all outside in the back yard and Dad started throwing the ball for me to catch. I was having an exceptionally good time playing the game. He wanted to see what speed I ran at naturally and if I was hopping or using all four legs. He noticed that I ran to catch the ball and that I used all four legs. Ten minutes later, he noticed that I had gotten tired and needed to stop and rest, and that's when we stopped playing that game. There was no escaping his gaze, either.

The next day, Mom and I had a good long walk at a quick pace for fifty minutes. In the beginning I was hopping a little and she had to slow me down by gently pulling on the lead and saying, "Slow down, Joey," though pulling on the lead was more effective. After a while I used all four legs even when we were going at a fast walk. Whether I was walking on sod or on the sidewalk, I was comfortable. But then again, it wasn't my custom to indicate when I was in pain.

I liked these walks with Mom and I liked that they were becoming more and more frequent.

"Joey, use four legs," I became accustomed to hearing Dad command me. And I would. Mom still tried to teach me the word *slowly*. But no matter how she said it, that one just never caught on. Whether I was out with Mom or Dad, both of them were looking at the muscles on my left side, the injured side, then looking at the muscles on my right side, and comparing the two.

Months of being so closely scrutinized no longer bothered me, if only because all this physical training was lots of fun.

Yet I was agitated. There was no substitute for the real thing. Sometimes at night I would be dreaming, my legs kicking wildly and working like pistons, and Mom or Dad would wake me up and pat my back. "You're dreaming. Calm down, puppy. Go back to sleep."

A CLASSY REUNION

One of those nights as I lay in my bed, Mom said something to me like, "Go to sleep, Joey. Tomorrow will be a big day" but I didn't really get what she was saying.

"It's going to be a cold run tomorrow," Dad said as he turned in.

I had become accustomed to awakening in the morning to see him wearing his running shoes and shorts and leaving home without me, but I still suffered a little each time I witnessed it. From inside the home the following morning, I again heard the patter of his feet heading down the front walkway to the road where it then stopped, the faint *beep beep* of his watch, and then the patter of his feet heading down the road and trailing off into silence. After a long silence, I heard the patter of his feet return, getting louder and louder, and then stopping while he checked his watch to see how long he'd been running.

Our morning walk had by now increased to about two miles: one mile along the Carriage Lane down to Bullough's Pond, a long, beautiful and bucolic pond with a rushing waterfall where Dad used to let me chase the geese on our morning runs because he knew that they would be airborne long before I could do them any harm, and then one mile back up the big long hill again to our home. It was fully bright out during these walks. I hadn't seen any foxes or coyotes in a long time, although plenty of bunnies would stop hopping when we walked by and would wait, with their backs turned to us, until we'd passed. Back home, I was given my morning treat, and soon afterwards Dad went off for the day and I was home alone with Mom. The morning began well enough, but I conceded that the remainder of the afternoon was going to be unspectacular.

I spent the late morning reclining on my bed, my front paws stretched out and cradling my head. I was alternating between sleeping and sulking but I was alert enough to detect anything out of the normal. Then anything occurred. New sounds came from outside, voices, cars, very near, scents very near. Mom left me and went out the front door to be a part of it but I couldn't see what. Surely this was not a visit from Animal Control.

When Mom came back inside, I could smell a dog all over her hands and arms. Not just any dog. *Didn't I know this dog?* I kept sniffing for more and more information. She was female. *Where was she? Would she be happy to see me? And why did I have to wait here, inside?* This time, the big wooden door was open but the inner glass door was closed. I could see through that inner glass door to the outside, however, and there on the sidewalk she sat, squarely and properly.

Mom snapped my lead onto my collar and slowly allowed me outside to the walkway. But I was not content to stop there. I tugged at the lead as hard as I possibly could to get closer to our special guest.

Mom said "Joey, sit" and I knew she meant business. It was a struggle for me and my struggle became our struggle, a struggle pitting me against Mom. Annoyed and firm, she called out, "Joey, you're so strong. Now *sit!*"

I finally sat on the walkway in front of our front door. Our guest, still sitting on the sidewalk, was just a little smaller than me. She was also a Lab. I had seen her before. I had met her before. For a few moments, she and I just looked at each other. She was feeling very uncomfortable in my territory. I wanted to get closer to her, however, and tried, again unsuccessfully, to extend the lead.

Meanwhile, our guest also had a mom and our two moms were saying things like "Good boy" and "Good girl," a nearly futile attempt to keep me calm and obedient and to keep the other dog well-behaved. I strained to obey.

Just at that moment, Al, one of our family friends, came casually walking along the sidewalk, heading for us and all the excitement. Al, like Mary the mail carrier, also had a pocketful of treats. He went over to this other dog and they made friends, which made her feel more comfortable. However, it made me more anxious because now there were three in the other group, which is where all the fun and the pocketsful of treats were, but only my Mom and me in my group, and no treats.

Soon, Mom let out the lead which allowed me to approach the sidewalk. When I got there, she again said, "Sit" and gave my lead to Al, who is pretty strong and made sure we two dogs remained separated.

Then there was a momentary silence.

"Joey, this is Rosie, your sister. Rosie, this is Joey, your brother." Honestly, this was very difficult for me and was becoming more difficult by the moment. I wasn't interested in the introductions. I was working hard to get closer to Rosie, Rosie was working hard to get closer to me, Al was working hard to restrain me, Rosie's mom was working hard to restrain Rosie, and my Mom was working hard saying, "Joey, sit. Joey, wait" to a dog who was really conflicted about obeying anybody at this very moment.

As my sister and I fought to inch closer toward each other, our moms finally decided that it was time to allow the next big step. Did they really have to drag this out?

Rosie allowed me to lick her face a little. It had been years but I wanted to take care of her! Together we two little siblings had squirmed in the same whelping pool where we opened our eyes and had our first views of the world. Together we had pushed our way over and through a pile of puppies to find and be nourished by Mother Cocoa's milk. We had played and cuddled together, learned to eat food and drink from water bowls, and learned to chew on small trees and to dig our teeth into our human family's t-shirts – and pull! We were now full-grown dogs, with families of our own, but I still wanted to take care of her.

From my point of view, this could have gone on forever! Then voices in unison drowned out my own thoughts, saying, "That's good enough for now. Let's maybe start walking soon. We don't want to do too much too fast. We have lots of time; let's not push it." With that, our moms pulled us apart again.

"Let's go in this direction," Mom decided, and off we headed toward the Carriage Lane, Rosie first and setting the pace, me following, and Al going his own way.

I, of course, wanted to race on ahead and be right on pace with Rosie, but she seemed uncomfortable with me so close behind her. She kept turning around and showing me her teeth. She wasn't smiling; she was letting me know she was annoyed. I couldn't take a hint. Mom kept pulling on my lead to slow me down, working very hard at this, and it was getting exhausting for her, so halfway down the block she said, "How about if Joey and I go first, and Rosie and you follow." So we all reversed places. This system worked pretty well.

All of this was new territory for Rosie and she was doing pretty well – as long as I was ahead of her and not turning back to stop and play with her, which was a challenge for me. There were some rules to this play date but these were certainly not my rules. We kept this up all down our block to the end, then turned left and continued along that block until we turned left again, and so on, and so on, until we ended up back home, where we stopped and rested. Although it was not a particularly long walk, it took up a lot of energy, with me tugging ahead on the lead all the time and Mom holding me back, so Mom took me inside to allow me to drink while Rosie's mom set out Rosie's very own water bowl right there on the sidewalk. Boy, this mom came prepared! Soon I was ready for another lap around another block. Off we all went, this time we headed in a different direction, Mom and me leading the way and Rosie and her mom following.

"Oh, two chocolates!" exclaimed people who passed us and enjoyed seeing how much alike we two looked. Then of course my sister and I had to stop and wait while our moms did a lot of talking.

Shortly after this, our moms decided for us that this was enough for our first walk together. I could have kept on going but I wasn't the one making the decisions here.

Back in front of our home, I kissed and licked my sister, telling her how much I liked her. Rosie wasn't much in the mood for being kissed right then and snarled, which startled me and shook my expectations. The moms decided to respect Rosie's wishes and made sure we were separated.

Then Mom got out her bag of treats, gave me a treat and said, "Good boy" and Rosie's mom gave Rosie a treat and said, "Good girl." Then Mom gave me another treat and Rosie's mom gave Rosie another treat. Then Mom gave Rosie a treat and said, "Good girl" and Rosie's mom tried to hand me a treat but instead dropped it on the ground and Rosie got to the treat before I had a chance to. Then Rosie's mom gave me a treat and said, "Good boy." Treats were everywhere and Mom became confused as to who was a girl and who was a boy. But above all, Rosie and I were happy that day, Mom's promise had been fulfilled and at least part of our family had become reunited, and the love that Mother Cocoa had nurtured in us had returned to embrace our newly extended family, even if my sister did occasionally display her front teeth.

IN DEEP WATER

The St. John's Water Dog, a dog from Labrador that eventually became the Labrador Retriever, was a great swimmer. Its paws, which developed into the Labrador's paws, were webbed, a characteristic which made, and makes, us great swimmers. Our tails, strong and long, were developed to be rudders, to steer us while swimming, and my tail was particularly strong. We were designed with two coats – a waxy and wiry undercoat to keep us warm and a waterproof top coat to keep us warm and dry in the cold waters off Labrador. My Mother Cocoa had been a dedicated swimmer and had delighted in jumping off the dock and swimming in the lake by her home in Connecticut. I had every reason to love swimming in deep water, but it terrified me.

Crystal Lake is located not too far from our home, and on numerous warm and sunny days Mom had taken me there. She and I would walk along the water's edge and we'd step into the water, further and further out, to where it would be up to my knees or sometimes the bottom of my belly. She would cup her hands and gently pour the warm sparkling water on my back. Then she'd walk out a little further with me. "So far so good," she would think and "Good boy," she would say. Then, as soon as it got just a little deeper the terror overtook me and I would heave myself up onto my hind legs, raising my chest onto the air, thrash my arms in the water spewing water all about, and grab onto Mom's arms, shoulders or neck, anything I could grab hold of with my paws, and not let go.

"Ouch!" she would scream, as my thick toenails scraped along her skin, leaving large red tracks down her arms and chest. "Joey, it's okay. It's fine. It's only water. Ouch!"

Then she would try to push me off her, calm me down, return me to the shallow part of the water, and gently instill confidence in me. "Joey! Good boy!" After a brief wait, step by slow step we would calmly enter the water, slowly walking toward the distant shore, my body slowly becoming submerged in the warm water, and at some moment once again terror would surge within me and I would thrash at the water with my front legs, as if trying to fight a demon; my two hind legs now bore all my weight as I would again raise my chest up above the water and stand so that Mom and I were about eye to eye. I would lunge at her, trying to get my paws onto her shoulders to steady me as high above the water as possible, and she would again cry out, "Ouch! Joey, calm down! Ouch, Joey, Joey, *Shhhhh*, it's okay, it's okay. It's only water. "

At night, Mom would show Dad her wounds. "Do you see what he did to me? Look at these marks and scratches all over me!"

But Mom never quit. Every new summer she would try again, driving me over to Crystal Lake on a warm summer day, entering the water with me, one step at a time, hoping that this year I would forget all about my fear of water – my deep fear of deep water. Each year she would get a little closer to her goal of my swimming out into deep water. "Joey, you're a dog. You're a Labrador Retriever, aren't you? I just don't get it."

There *was* something at the lake – and in the lake – that I was very interested in, however, and that was the other dogs. I was also interested in the children. And this too became a problem because if Mom was lucky enough to get me into the deep water without thrashing at her, I would always swim out to the other dogs and try to play with them in the water, or swim to the children and try to play with them in the water.

"Joey, no," Mom would scream. She would even swim out to pull my collar or lead if it was still attached and, gently pulling on the lead or collar, direct me away from the children or the other dogs.

One summer day the children who were playing in the water learned to play along with me. I was in deep water just about up to my chest when the children gripped one end of my lead and, as I headed desperately and resolutely toward the shore with all my might, I pulled them toward shore while they laughed and floated, in tow, through the water behind me.

After I was hit by the car and the splint removed, my parents had another idea, which I was soon to discover. The idea, the game, was called Physical Therapy.

One afternoon Mom and Dad put a new harness on me, something that wrapped all the way around my body and that I had to step into, and packed up the car with my lead and towels – and then me. In a little while we three were at my beloved lake. We took a nice walk along the walking path that was elevated slightly above the level of the water and we all ended up at a quiet cove at one end of the lake, where a wide grassy field sloped into a long and narrow field of sand. There, Mom took her end of my lead and headed straight for the water and so I followed.

Dad waited on the elevated path while Mom and I got our feet wet walking along the water's edge for a while. The sunlight felt good, the warm water felt great. Mom tugged on the lead for me to go in deeper. She said, "Joey, come. Let's swim!"

I walked with her until the water was up to my knees and then we turned around and walked back to our starting point by Dad. Soon I wanted to go in again, this time deeper. Mom let the lead out to its longest and let me swim out ahead of her. Eventually I turned around toward shore to come back in. We played this game for a while.

"Maybe this is your year, Joey," she whispered, encouraged that I might become a swimmer after all, encouraged that she wouldn't end up with deep scratches on her arms, neck, and chest.

Then we played a new game. Mom and I walked out, then she continued past me and further out into the water and once there, she said, "Joey, come" and I swam hard toward her. "Joey's swimming," I could hear Mom calling. I was nervous but I was feeling great, I was feeling strong, and the warm water was comforting. As soon as I had just about reached Mom, suddenly I realized I was in deep water and not able to see the distant shore. All I saw was a dark mass in front of me. I quickly pivoted and steered myself to face Dad and the nearest shore. Panic abated but I was determined to reach solid ground. I paddled as hard as I could until I reached Dad – and safety – and relaxed. From there I turned around, saw Mom out there in the water, heard Mom out there calling, "Joey, come!" and decided to go back in the water and walk or swim toward her as she beckoned and wiggled her fingers to urge me forward and into the water, which I did. For at least a few moments, I was unaware of how fearful I was of swimming.

We played this game again and again, back and forth, back and forth. This was not a bad game, all in all, though eventually I always became distracted by other dogs, which is about when both my parents agreed with each other and said, "I think that's enough for the first day" and happy to stay on land and dry off I certainly was.

The next time we went to Crystal Lake, Mom threw out a tennis ball, and I was supposed to go into the water after my ball. I started to. I was in the water, well on my way to the ball, breathing hard, but then my feet were unable to feel the ground beneath me. The surface of the water appeared to be a gigantic black hole. Frightened, I steered myself around to face and reach the nearby shoreline and plant my feet firmly on the solid ground where I had started out.

"Okay, Joey, this isn't going to work. We're going to have to try something else," Mom said. Standing in water up to her waist, she called me and then gently lifted me up by the strap of my harness that ran along my spine so that my feet were no longer touching the bottom of the lake and I was facing our point of entry, our closest beach. I began paddling my feet beneath me, eager to reach the shore. I was working hard – but I didn't seem to be getting any closer. I was paddling and huffing and puffing, but still I remained as far from shore as I had started out. "Good boy, Joey. You're swimming," she repeated over and over, while I got absolutely nowhere.

In a weightless environment, my legs – my injured leg in particular – were getting a great workout without the pressure of my leg beating against the hard pavement or ground.

Every once in a while Mom let go of the harness and let me really swim – on my own to shore to give me the impression that there really was some purpose to all this. There, I relaxed a bit and, quickly distracted, sniffed around. Before long, we began our exercise in deep water again, with Mom holding the harness as I faced the shore and paddled my legs and webbed feet beneath the surface of the water and went nowhere.

With this regimen every few days, my legs eventually became stronger, even though my fear of deep water lingered.

I learned quickly that if Mom put my harness on me, I was going to have a good time. One such day, she and I drove to the cove as usual. She acclimated me to the warm water and to the depth of the water. She was lifting me up by the strap of my harness, the water was massaging my weakened legs and muscles, and I was paddling as hard as I could, breathing hard and keeping my head above water, when a man whom I'd never seen before suddenly appeared on shore close to the water's edge and partly hidden by the overhanging of the trees.

This man was not Dad.

This man, wearing a dark suit and holding something in his hands, just stood there looking at us. Behind him on the road was a black and white car. He could have been a nice person but he was awfully serious, something told me.

"Hello, Officer," Mom called in her typically friendly voice, though with some reservation. To me, she whispered, "Joey, stop. Stop. *Shhhh.* Come with me."

"You must leave the water immediately," the man called.

Mom carried me through the water to where it was shallower and I could stand. "Why?" Mom asked. "What law are we violating?"

"My orders have it that nobody is to be in the water." The man gripped something in his hands. For once in my life I wasn't trying to make friends with somebody.

"But I'm just helping my dog with his physical therapy. He was hit by a car."

"I have my orders," the man repeated.

"But what law are we violating? I'm not swimming. I'm just helping him to exercise his broken leg."

"My orders are to get everybody out of the water."

"Including my dog? He's even on a lead!"

I take it that Mom saw that she wasn't going to get anywhere with this conversation because she got out of the water with me following close behind, grabbed her towel and dried me off. And then we left the area. Though I had begun to love my physical therapy lessons a little bit and I loved the lake a lot more, my swim and physical therapy trips to the lake were to come to an end.

Late one afternoon, Mom was walking me along the Carriage Lane toward the Pond, in the direction of the setting sun. Way up ahead, I saw another dog running solo. His freedom ignited jealousy. I couldn't tell which direction this dog was heading in until a few moments later, when he appeared larger and heading toward us. This hardly concerned me, but it did concern Mom. Suddenly she seemed very jumpy.

As the dog got closer to us, she called out, "It's a Retriever." *Who was she talking to? I hate when I don't know whom she's talking to.* Then she called, "Come." I'm sure this was directed to me. But *Come where? And why?*

The dog continued running toward us, mouth open and panting. Was he hot, thirsty, tired, or happy to see us? *Could I play with him?* Mom moved over to stand on the grassy berm that separated the Carriage Lane from the four-lane avenue where I had been hit by a car and where I never ever was to go.

Suddenly she called out, "Puppy, come! Stay close to me!" *Was she talking to me?* She was holding me on a very short lead so that I was only inches from her. Then the excitable dog came right up to us and scouted us out. Now Mom wanted me to play with the dog a little but not too much. She loosened up my lead a little. She thought aloud. "He's a Lab. Labs are friendly. But I don't know what to do. Should I call the police?" *Did she expect an answer from me?* She knew that if she telephoned my friend Officer O'Connell, he would be notified, or maybe that she would just get a recorded message. "I can't call the police while the dog is still running."

What was I supposed to do? How was I supposed to help?

In a moment, the Retriever calmed down and Mom held out her open hand, palm up, for the dog to smell. He approved. Then she got even closer and looked to see if there was a tag on his collar. There wasn't. I was all confused and didn't know if I should play, sit, stand, or what.

The Retriever then suddenly picked up running again, continuing in the same direction. I wanted to follow him and apparently Mom had the same idea but maybe for different reasons. She was still talking incomprehensibly into the air, trying to follow the dog and to hold onto me as I was tugging and tugging on my lead all at the same time. The more agitated she became, the more excited I became. The dog was, by then, significantly past us, crossing the next road and heading east down another. As we saw him receding from view, Mom called, "Joey, come. Let's go this way." *Good. At least now I know what is expected of me.* I followed as commanded. The dog ran down the sidewalk of the next block and we ran too. He stopped at a home, ran down the driveway and over to the side door. We caught up and stopped on the sidewalk. Nothing and nobody moved. Then the dog went to the front door and sat. Mom tied my lead to a post on the lawn, said, "Stay here. Wait here. Good boy," and of course used her new hand signals to make her point, and walked up the wooden steps of that home and pressed the doorbell.

In a minute the door opened and a man came out. "Max!" he exclaimed, surprised, and Max disappeared into the home while the man remained standing.

Then Mom started pointing at me, being still tied to the post, and told the man the story of my getting free and getting hit by a car on the same avenue where Max was found running loose. The man was nice and he listened. Then he spoke.

"I had Max in the back yard and on his lead. I didn't know he'd gotten free. I don't know how he got free." Yeah, Mom thought, pointing to me again. Same story. And I wasn't about to offer up any suggestions.

This is why, Mom supposed, Officer O'Connell is such a busy man.

WAKE-UP CALL

"Joey, wake up! Wake up! You're having a bad dream!"

I woke up with a jolt and in the darkness and a daze, I was staring blankly at Mom and Dad and once I was comforted and aware of where I was and whom I was with, my muscles slowly relaxed, I lay my head back down to rest on my bed and I exhaled. "Joey, are you running in your dreams? Are you playing with the other dogs? It's okay; it's okay. Go back to sleep now." Mom's voice was soothing. After settling down, I went off to sleep, and to my dreams, once again.

More and more often in the middle of the night I'd feel somebody petting my head or shaking my body to soothe or arouse me. There in the dark would be Mom and Dad staring at me, a far cry from what was happening in my dreams.

It had been twelve weeks since my surgery, four months since my injury, and even longer since I'd gone running with Dad. This hiatus was taking its toll on me.

Gradually, my undercoat, which had been shaved for surgery and the placement of medical patches, had fully grown in while the top coat remained bare but slowly beginning to fill in. The scars and bare spots along my leg and belly were still visible to people who still stopped to observe, but were diminishing. I was limping less and less. I was also getting more and more signs of time passing – grey hairs under my nose and around my chin, and now grey hairs even on my legs and around my paws – which many people commented on. I certainly was getting lots of rest, and once again the neighborhood children came by our home to pet and play with me. When I walked, I was always using four legs and was becoming strong enough to pull Mom, on the other end of the lead, up the big long hill when she and I were out for a walk and she became tired.

And so the new question around our home was, "How will we know that it's okay to take Joey running?"

Then one day my parents got the answer they sought.

"It's time for him to start again," the doctor had answered my parents. "Keep an eye on him and if you notice anything unusual, rest him for a day then try again."

The following morning Dad woke up early, as usual, just as the light was breaking and the birds were starting their songs, and the smell of Dad's coffee filled the air. Dad went out – without me – running, I presume, and I fell back asleep. As usual, Mom, who'd been sleeping in her bed this whole time, didn't stir through it all.

I could hear Dad return home from his run and go into the kitchen to have some breakfast. Then I heard him come upstairs and open the bedroom door. He walked over to where I lay in my own bed and whispered, "Joey, let's go."

I raised my head, stood up, yawned, stretched my front legs, then my rear legs, pulled myself forward with my front feet, and sneezed. Then I headed downstairs, following Dad, into the kitchen, where I had a drink of some fresh water. Dad always filled my water bowl with fresh water in the morning. In a while, he went to the front door and I followed. He grabbed for the lead.

We were, in an instant, outside to begin my morning walk. The morning light was just about how it was that day when I had been hit by the car, six months earlier. Dad and I walked for a while in the stillness and the freshness of the early morning, heading toward the Carriage Lane. "Look, Joey. A bunny." I didn't even look. It was a little cool out and our pace was comfortable. Now and then another runner passed us by.

We were well on our way when, with no warning, Dad quickened his pace from walking to a running gait, stretching the lead to its fullest. The lead tugged at my neck. I looked at Dad's back; he wasn't waiting for me to catch up. He wasn't even looking back at me to see how I was doing. There was only one thing for me to do: to speed up and match his gait. And I did. We were moving smoothly side by side when he sped up some more – and I sped up some more. He continued down the block; I remained right by his side. An ecstatic energy exploded throughout my body and propelled me forward.

At the end of that block, Dad stopped, and I stopped. He looked at his watch, then at me, turned around and started walking toward home. I looked at him, turned around and started walking toward home. I was tired. But this was no dream that I would wake up from. I'd sought to regain the familiarity and solidarity of our old companionship – and here it was.

All that day, he and Mom were looking at me walk to make sure I wasn't limping.

That evening, Mom and Dad were sitting around the kitchen table and eating, and I was close by, when Mom gave me some news.

"Joey, I heard from Dr. Kiko today. He has a message for you. He says 'Joey, I hope to see you again, just not at the hospital.'" There wasn't too much for me to do in response, other than to look attentively, wag my tail, and hope my parents would give me a little food from what they were eating. Whatever they were eating was always more desirable than what was in my food bowl. "Maybe he'll see you at the Boston Marathon!"

The next morning before daybreak, Dad got up as usual, dressed in his running clothes, went downstairs, had his coffee, took his morning run – without me – and came home and had his breakfast. He then tiptoed up the stairs and into the bedroom – where Mom lay asleep in her bed and I lay awake on mine, my head rested but my eyes following Dad's every movement – and once again whispered, "Joey, let's go."

We walked to the Carriage Lane. Outside, a few squirrels scampered up trees as we passed by. The morning light was just beginning to shine on us and the glow of the streetlights was beginning to appear pale against the iridescent sky. I was warmed up. At the beginning of the next block, once again without warning, Dad sped up. I responded. This time he didn't stop or slow down at all, though. For one whole block we ran side by side. It was the longest block I had ever run. At the end, Dad slowed down and I slowed down, and together we walked slowly for one more block.

Again, Dad sped up and again I responded. This continued for about one complete block, running past bushes, trees, homes. One whole block! Then he noticed it. I was hopping on three legs.

He immediately slowed down so that we were just walking, and we walked at a slow pace all the way home. My head really hung down low to the ground, but I felt great and my tail never ceased wagging.

All day my parents were looking at me, once again. Was I using all four legs? Was I limping? For my part, I slept a lot that day.

Sometimes it takes practice to do what comes naturally.

Each of the next few mornings, when I heard the sound of Dad's footsteps coming up the stairs, I was confused and unsure about what to expect. When he opened the bedroom door and stuck his head in and whispered, "Joey, wake up. Joey, come," I obeyed. I followed him downstairs but the anticipation was agonizing. *Would we walk? Would we run?*

One morning stood out. Dad dressed in his running clothes and told me to come downstairs with him. He poured me fresh water. Then he clipped the lead on my collar and opened the front door to allow us to exit and we immediately entered the vast darkness, beauty, serenity. Tiny dots of orange light were dangling all in a row, high above the roads. It was too late for the cicadas and too early for the birds or the bunnies. It was too early for the other runners and dogs. But it wasn't too early for us.

Dad and I walked up our road then turned right along the Carriage Lane. We had the Carriage Lane to ourselves. In the stillness, we walked along the promenade for a while, continuing to where it sloped gently downhill.

At the bottom of the long hill, Dad turned to walk in the direction of the pond. With the pond now barely visible, he picked up speed. I did too. He maintained that speed, and I did too. The pond where the ducks lay and incubated their eggs and where ducks swam and took off and landed in the glassy water lay to our left. We ran past the spot where the turtles lay their eggs and kept running. I was even slightly ahead of Dad and turned my head back every now and then to keep my eyes on him and see what he was going to do, what he wanted me to do, and where he wanted me to go.

We rounded the corner to continue bordering the pond, the glassy water now shiny from the morning light bounding off of it, and ran over a small bridge that crossed over the creek that was fed by the pond. We ran past the *whoosh* of the waterfall. I was on pace and breathing hard. We met up with a larger and longer road that went uphill. The sky, the road, the trees, everything was becoming more and more visible, more and more bright. Dad and I ran on. Then we encountered the Carriage Lane again where Mom had shown me the statue of the two runners who probably didn't run with their dogs, and we turned left and continued up the hill we had come down, now toward home. Up and up the hill we raced, the berm now on my right, until we reached the top of the hill. Then we turned onto our road, still running, and ran up to our home, which was now bathed in the first full light of the day. Exhausted I was, for sure.

Luckily, inside, there was still plenty of fresh water for me in my bowl. And of course one treat waiting for me.

It's a good thing I was running with Dad because I wouldn't have known when to stop and rest my muscles. I wouldn't know when to stop and drink water. But my Dad knew.

INHERITANCE

One sunny day while Mom and I were home, Al, with his pocketful of treats, came by. Mom looked serious, and she sounded serious. I wasn't going to get a treat from Al this time.

"Al, you have a dog; you have a Lab. Maybe you can help me. I need to do things differently. I need to get Joey out of the house more often. He runs in the morning with Phil, but then all the rest of the day he's cooped up with me or he's cooped up alone at home while I'm out. Even when he's in the yard, he's fairly constrained. He's not with other dogs. He's never with other dogs. I just don't think this is helping. This isn't what he needs. Can you give me any ideas?"

And that wasn't all. Mom knew that if she left me alone outside there was a chance that I'd do again what I'd done before. "We're *not* going to go through this again," she added, sounding slightly tired.

But she also didn't want to leave me alone *inside* the home. She and Dad wanted my muscles to get back to how strong they were when Dad and I would run regularly. She also wanted me to be happy.

The days of summer had been winding down; new and different colors and scents had taken the place of the summer colors and scents. Often when Mom was going out, she would stand there in the hall in front of the door, hold her keys and her bag, and look straight-faced at me wagging my tail and looking at her. I would station myself as close to the door as possible.

There would be a pause in Mom's demeanor. When the days were cooler, she would then say, to my dismay, "Joey, it's too cold in the car for you today. I can't leave you alone in a cold car." And when the days were very hot, she would then say, "Joey, it's too hot in the car for you today. I can't leave you alone in a hot car." So on those days, despite my drama, I remained, regretfully, in our home and alone.

"So Al," Mom said on this day, with a heavy sigh, "Where do you take Lucky? I need some ideas." Lucky had come to play with me once or twice a long time ago.

"Have you tried Cat Rock Park?" he answered.

I recognized the good sign when, later that week, Mom had me step into my harness, and she filled a little bag with treats and a container with water. The day was not too cold or too hot: I eagerly took my place by the window in the backseat of the car. We drove and drove and, with the window open, I sniffed at the air that blew across my face, and sniffed some more. Where was she going? I didn't care. We drove and drove some more, further than usual. There were fewer and fewer cars. I could tell that we were getting closer to some place where I really wanted to be, some place made exactly for me.

Cat Rock Park. Even in the parking lot we were surrounded by quiet and stillness and powerful scents. I just couldn't wait to get out of the car, although I had to. Mom got out of the car, came around to my side and opened the door. I was ready to jump out. "No, not yet, Joey," she said. This was taking too long. She then clipped the lead onto my harness and allowed me to jump out of the car, closed the car door behind me, and started walking, lead in hand, away from the road, toward a thick canopy of trees. I accompanied her to where she found a narrow path that led away from the car and there unclipped the lead from my harness, liberating me from her control.

Here the trees were so tall and so plentiful that I could barely see the sky. There was a wide clearing between the dense foliage, along which we could easily walk, and I was allowed to go anywhere I wanted that my four legs would carry me. Dogs had been here before me, many dogs. As we got further along that trail and deeper into these woods, I could stop and sniff by the side of the trail, or I could run up ahead leaving Mom far behind, stop, turn around, and run back to her. Or I could explore some bush, some leaves while Mom walked up ahead, barely looking back at me, and then I could run up ahead and catch up to her. She was relaxed and said hardly a word. As in the quiet and stillness of this path in this blessed woodland, I found my place. I could almost hear the call and feel the approval of my father and his father and his father and mother, champion hunters all.

A babbling stream lay ahead and its waters called out. A little footbridge that crossed over the stream held no interest for me. The waters did. There was a small descent to the stream that had me maneuvering various sizes of rocks. Mom didn't remind me that I was supposed to be afraid of water, or that I was recovering from injury. Instead, she encouraged me on ahead, saying "Go go go." As she arrived by the stream, she nudged me toward the cool water's edge. I had no fear this time. I had no concern, though I can't say the same for Mom, for at the water's edge she clipped my lead back onto my collar. Despite this, I walked right down and into the water, oblivious to her, lured in by the tale that the flowing water carried within it. Mom perched herself on a rock and halted. I kept going farther and farther into increasingly deeper and deeper water, along my way carefully exploring from rock to rock when necessary.

Each large and small rock that lay in the water protruding above the sparkling water's surface presented itself as a small stepping stone, a small platform for my route. Step by step I continued; I kept my focus and soon was halfway across the stream and halfway to the other side. Water rushed all around me. There were fewer and fewer rocks to step on and more and more water, rushing faster and faster. I had to calculate where my next safe landing was to be. Occasionally I looked back at Mom to catch her eye but had to be careful not to disturb my balance. Mom just stood there looking at me.

The steep banks of the other side seemed far away but not out of reach. I just had to figure out how to get there.

The small rock I was balancing on offered temporary respite, but I couldn't stay here all day. I hadn't yet figured out my next step, my new move, when I felt the tug of my lead. This was Mom's way of telling me I couldn't go any further. I turned and carefully made my way back across the water, retracing my path from rock to rock to where she stood and waited for me. Then suddenly she entered the stream, slowing moving toward me, crossing the rushing waters of the stream, allowing me to go forward again. She followed close behind me every step of the way. I didn't slip or fall once. Together we forged the rushing waters.

Safely at the other side, I found the opening between the bushes and climbed the steep and rocky stream bank to where it leveled off and met up with the trail again, and so did Mom. I shook myself off. It was time to move on. There, Mom again unclipped the lead. I was once more on my own. I wandered, explored, stopped, smelled, and delighted. Maybe the memories of my father Buckfold Classical Sir, my grandfathers and my great-grandfathers, champion hunters all, were visiting Mom too.

In the days when I would try to dig my way under the fence and get out of the back yard, I was alone and trying to escape from one world into another. Today, Mom was even accompanying me in that world.

Soon we two moved along, down a wide path with more tall trees and full bushes off to either side. Fallen leaves softened our footsteps. When I stopped to sniff, Mom stopped. When I started moving again, Mom moved. When I stopped again, she stopped. Then I galloped as far ahead as I could, stopped and turned around, saw she was way back, and galloped excitedly back to her. She hardly said a word but smiled and kept on walking. I was overwhelmed with life and with freedom. Eventually we arrived at a juncture where we turned left and then went down another narrower path. The scents told me that so many dogs had been here along this path. They told me that dogs had been along this path just a little while before I arrived.

At the end of that path we beheld a large clearing, the sky became visible once more and so did a body of water so large that I could barely see across to the other side. In the water was one dog who kept trying to catch a tennis ball that his dad, standing on the shore, was throwing again and again into the water. As usual I was interested in the dog. Mom clipped the lead back onto my collar and into the water I went, Mom tugging gently on my lead whenever I threatened to climb onto the swimming dog. She broke her silence.

"Joey, you can't jump onto dogs who are swimming in the water. You'll hurt them. Joey, no!" Rebuke me she tried, but only the tugging of the lead allowed my new friend to swim and

play freely. Soon that dog left and once again Mom unclipped my harness from the lead and I had the whole body of water to myself.

For a while.

Dogs and more dogs (and some people) soon started arriving. Groups of two dogs (and a person). Then groups of five dogs (and a person). Then even a group of ten dogs (and a person)! Some dogs swam, some dogs played on the dry ground with each other. I had a good time finding and making new friends, especially making friends with the dogs on dry ground. Then all those dogs left and again this serene wonderland returned to us, alone.

Mom took me for one final swim in the large lake; it was one last opportunity to exercise my injured leg and get it moving. This time, she entered the water with me and encouraged me to swim. The water felt good. As usual, I started swimming out into deep water and when I couldn't see the other side and the water's surface looked to me like a big black hole, I panicked, turned around, and trying as hard as I could to keep my head above water, headed for the closest shore, the shore I knew. But I was swimming.

Back on the dry land, Mom dried me off with a towel she'd brought along. We slowly retraced our steps along the wooded trail, meeting other dogs and groups of dogs, and stopping to play along the way. Mom was surprisingly silent, and I liked it. I sniffed at the babbling creek as it meandered through the woodland, but this time Mom and I crossed over the little wooden bridge that traversed the babbling creek where it was deep and wide. We continued to where we could see the sky again and arrived back at our car. But the good time didn't end there. Mom gave me treats and set my water bowl on the ground, filled it with fresh water that she'd brought, and said, "Joey, drink water." I did, and then we headed back home.

This was it. I was now initiated into a long and proud line of Retrievers, bred to run, to retrieve, to cross streams and valleys, to roam and sniff, to be a friend of men and women (and other dogs) and to be obedient and gentle. Today I was my father's son and my grandfather's grandson, my great-grandfather's great-grandson. And Mom was happy to let me just be who I am. At night time, Mom told the story of our adventure to a very proud Dad who gave me a pat on my head.

Later, when it approached bedtime, he said, "Okay, Joey; let's go upstairs. Up you go! It's going to be a cold run tomorrow morning." And up the stairs the two of us climbed, the sounds of many footsteps being heard as we ascended, to feel completely satisfied with this day, and to be ready for a new one.

My morning runs with Dad became more and more frequent. They also became longer, not quite but almost as long as the runs I used to know. Every morning now I awoke with hope, anticipating the welcome sound of Dad's feet coming up the stairs, opening the door to the bedroom, where I was once again allowed to sleep, and whispering, "Come on, Joey." I didn't know anything about it being early in the morning; I knew about it feeling right. I had my old friend back, and he did too.

Mom and I went to other outdoor areas too, where I was free from my lead and free to run and explore in nature's fields and hills and valleys for long stretches of time, where many other dogs were roaming and scampering free as well. On one of my walks in an extremely large off-lead woods, we had come upon two dogs with a man. These two dogs, Hudson and Sarge, and I had then run off into a beautiful meadow, enjoying a lovely and enthusiastic game of chase while Mom and this man looked on and talked. These were not the man's dogs, though. He was a dog group leader and Hudson and Sarge were part of the group.

At home, Mom started spending a lot of time contemplating. She would stop what she was doing, look at me, and contemplate. Compared to running outdoors, her contemplating was boring. Very boring. One afternoon, while we were in our back yard, she looked me and said, "Joey, I still don't know. What about a dog walker for you for the afternoons? Somebody who can take you out in the afternoons for a romp in the woods? I just think you need a lot more activity than your morning run with Dad and an occasional walk in the woods with me." She was talking to me. "Joey, would you like that? You could play with Hudson and Sarge a few times a week. You got along well with them. We can get you into their group. I think you just need to be with other dogs more often," she said. "That's what you need and I can't take you to the off-lead dog park as often as you need to go there." With that said, she contemplated a moment longer, and then picked up a ball and threw it past me to initiate a game of catch.

A few days later, a woman came over to our home to interview me. All seemed to be going well. She liked me. Mom was happy. "Joey, you're going to make new friends. You'll be able to express all your energy." Mom was pleased.

But one day Mom sounded sad when she said to Dad, "She can't take Joey. Her group leader quit and she can't take on any new clients..." Mom's frustration was increasing. "I'm sorry, Joey," she said to me. But I wasn't going to worry.

Another afternoon, I was home alone with Mom, and nothing was doing. I was bored. I had gotten used to all the daytime excitement of running and discovery, and here I was at home with Mom, and nothing was doing. Nothing at all. In the afternoon, Dad appeared. To my surprise and delight, Mom got my travel kit and put a few treats and poop bags in there, and filled a container with some water. Then she got my lead. I was crazed with anxiety over where we were going to go – and when. Dad, Mom and I got into the car and drove onto the highway. My window open, the wind blew fast and furiously over my face, offerings of scents and aroma, of lives and life. I could have been happy just being in the car all day. But no, we stopped. We stopped at a beautiful place, very large and open, and there was a still and very large lake here, very much larger than my beloved Crystal Lake. Very much larger than my Cat Rock Park! I hopped out of the car, felt the solid ground beneath my feet and breathed in the scents that enveloped me. Mom clipped the lead onto my collar and led me down, or rather I led her, to a narrow strip of sand that lined the water's edge, which we two then walked along. Dad followed close behind. The strip of sand opened up to a much wider and larger beach. Sky was everywhere above us. Nothing stood between the wind and me.

Soon, Mom unclipped the lead. I was unhindered. I ran along the shoreline away from my parents, and back down toward them. A thick grove of tall trees was set back against the sand and the water. I ran toward the trees in one direction, then back along the water in the other direction. The sand was soft, but cool. Whenever I stopped running, Mom would start running. I would run to catch up with and overcome her, and then run circles around her. Dad too ran the length of the beach, and I caught up with him and then ran ahead. I barked and laughed and played. The freedom, the movement, and the expanse excited my soul. Then Dad, Mom, and I walked, with me in the middle, to a nearby huge and open field with more grass than I had ever seen. Suddenly, Mom began to run, and I ran to catch up to her, except that I was very fast, much faster than she, and I was soon way ahead of her.

Soon the real races began.

Dad took off running across the expansive field into the distance, where sat a large hill covered with trees. When he was halfway there, I took off running to catch up with him and I even got a little ahead of him. I looked back at him – yes, he was still there, and he was still running. We reached the hill and ran up its slope, where we stopped briefly midway up. Then Dad headed back down the large hill and back across the vast field as quickly as he could, and I matched him. Back and forth we raced, side to side. We found many versions of this running game, and many ways to both win.

I was having a wonderful time with my family, joyous beyond anything I had ever imagined. In a while, my parents and I slowly walked back to the beach. Mom picked up a pinecone from the sand and threw it out into the water, and I ran into the water, up to my waist, picked the pinecone up with my mouth, brought it back to her, and lay it where the edge of the water met the dry sand. Dad then tried this game; he threw the pinecone into the water and, although it hadn't travelled very far, I swam out and brought the pinecone back to him. Then Mom threw it and I swam out and got it. Then Dad threw it and I swam out and got it. This was a good game.

"He's retrieving. He's actually retrieving," Mom called out with excitement in her voice, and a little disbelief as well.

RETURN

Today is a warm sunny day in the season of falling leaves. I have watched leaves fall from the trees and swirl on their way down. As a puppy, I used to try to catch the leaves. Now many of them cover the ground and many are still on the trees. Those that have fallen are now drying out so when I amble around our back yard, you can hear the *swoosh swoosh* of my legs pushing through the leaves or my turning them over with my nose. I could sit and relax in the sun but I find it more interesting to explore the smells on the ground and to keep moving. I begin my promenade along the perimeter of our yard, under the still-leafy bushes and hidden from Mom's surveying eyes.

Mom sits at the patio table having something to eat. She seems to be unaware of me. This is so unusual. All seems calm and relaxed. Perhaps she is wondering what new things and new places I will discover, and what new things and new places she will discover with me. Perhaps she is concerned about what new opportunities I will take advantage of, without my parents' permission.

I eventually emerge from the shadows of the leafy perimeter, nose to the ground and sneak a peek at Mom. She is getting up from the table. I raise my head toward her. She takes her plate and utensils, holds them with one hand and cleans the table with the other, then turns her back toward me and heads toward the porch door to go inside, carrying her plate and things. She is not saying "Joey, come inside." She is not even looking at me to assess the situation. She is not saying anything. She is willing to leave me here outside, all by myself. I'm not sure that I like this. I see it all happening. This worries me. Mom approaches and starts up the three steps to the door. She places her free hand on the door and pauses, turns her head, and takes a quick glance toward me.

I return the glance and stare at her, my ears now fully perked, my eyes open wide. I haven't moved through all this.

Mom. Are you going inside without me? Are you going to leave me here all alone? Don't leave me here all alone . . . and I stand up and gallop toward her, unaware of the crinkled and dried leaves that I am crunching beneath my feet as I race toward our home and my Mom's side.

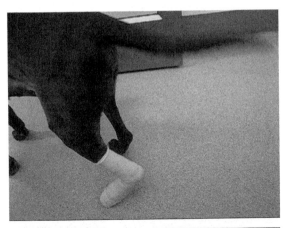

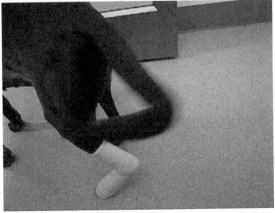

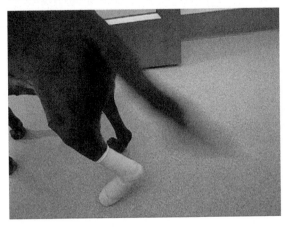

EPILOGUE

When I signed up to see Joey as my patient at our busy emergency hospital, I had no idea that that experience would later be chronicled in the pages of a book. I can say that during a rather intense week of hospitalization, I recognized that Jane and Joey were incredibly strong and magnetic personalities who I reluctantly said 'good bye' to when Joey was clearly on the mend. Interestingly, I've told parts of Joey's story many times over to friends and colleagues since that time, and now the full story is available to read.

Dogs Don't Look Both Ways will feel quite familiar to anyone who has lived with a dog that has boundless energy and curiosity, and an irrepressible gregarious nature. If dogs were not prone to forcing themselves into our families and our hearts, America's love affair with *the family dog* would look very different than it does. I have witnessed our collective human-animal bond grow exponentially in the last fifteen years, and Joey is the embodiment of why that has happened. In reading these pages, it is easy to see why dogs are thought of as man's best friend.

Kiko Bracker, DVM, DACVECC
Director, Emergency and Critical Care, Angell Animal Medical Center

ABOUT THE AUTHOR

Jane Hanser's poetry, essays, movie reviews and more have been published in numerous print and online journals. She has developed software to teach writing, authored an English grammar book and taught English as a Second Language at City University of New York. In her other life, she is involved in many and varied community activities, principally feeding the needy, bicycle and pedestrian safety, and literacy. She lives, works and plays in Newton, MA, but she wishes she had more time for play and spent less on work and mending fences. Joey's descriptions of her are, except for a few insignificant details of time and place, true and accurate.

Please visit us at www.dogsdontlookbothways.com.

by Jane Hanser

copyright 2009, 2012, 2014 Jane Hanser

ISBN 978-0-9915149-0-8

Library of Congress Control Number 2014902204

First Printing, 2014

Printed in the United States of America

IVY BOOKS an imprint of

Software for Students

Newton Centre, MA

info@dogsdontlookbothways.com

info@softwareforstudents.com

Front cover design and back cover design by

Jonathan D. Scott

Lotus Graphic Design

www.lotusgraphicdesign.com

Front cover photograph

www.markthomsonphoto.com

CPSIA information can be obtained
at www.ICGtesting.com
Printed in the USA
LVOW05*0214181116
513424LV00022BA/335/P